MW01675462

Villanova University

Villanova, Pennsylvania

Written by Sean Wright

Edited by Kelly Carey, Kimberly Moore, and Jon Skindzier

Layout by Jaime Myers

Additional contributions by Omid Gohari, Christina Koshzow, Chris Mason, Joey Rahimi, and Luke Skurman

College Prowler

ISBN # 1-4274-0210-8

ISSN # 1552-1540

Printed in the U.S.A.

www.collegeprowler.com

Last Updated 5/06/08

Special Thanks To: Babs Carryer, Andy Hannah, LaunchCyte, Tim O'Brien, Bob Sehlinger, Thomas Emerson, Andrew Skurman, Barbara Skurman, Bert Mann, Dave Lehman, Daniel Fayock, Chris Babyak, The Donald H. Jones Center for Entrepreneurship, Terry Slease, Jerry McGinnis, Bill Ecenberger, Idie McGinty, Kyle Russell, Jacque Zaremba, Larry Winderbaum, Roland Allen, Jon Reider, Team Evankovich, Lauren Varacalli, Abu Noaman, Mark Exler, Daniel Steinmeyer, Jared Cohon, Gabriela Oates, David Koegler, and Glen Meakem.

Bounce-Back Team: Claire Mitchell, Jim Saksa, and Jenna Cucco.

College Prowler®
5001 Baum Blvd.
Suite 750
Pittsburgh, PA 15213

Phone: 1-800-290-2682
Fax: 1-800-772-4972
E-Mail: info@collegeprowler.com
Web Site: www.collegeprowler.com

How this all started...

When I was trying to find the perfect college, I used every resource that was available to me. I went online to visit school websites; I talked with my high school guidance counselor; I read book after book; I hired a private counselor. Sure, this was all very helpful, but nothing really told me what life was like at the schools I cared about. These sources weren't giving me enough information to be totally confident in my decision.

In all my research, there were only two ways to get the information I wanted.

The first was to physically visit the campuses and see if things were really how the brochures described them, but this was quite expensive and not always feasible. The second involved a missing ingredient: the students. Actually talking to a few students at those schools gave me a taste of the information that I needed so badly. The problem was that I wanted more but didn't have access to enough people.

In the end, I weighed my options and decided on a school that felt right and had a great academic reputation, but truth be told, the choice was still very much a crapshoot. I had done as much research as any other student, but was I 100 percent positive that I had picked the school of my dreams?

Absolutely not.

My dream in creating *College Prowler* was to build a resource that people can use with confidence. My own college search experience taught me the importance of gaining true insider insight; that's why the majority of this guide is composed of quotes from actual students. After all, shouldn't you hear about a school from the people who know it best?

I hope you enjoy reading this book as much as I've enjoyed putting it together. Tell me what you think when you get a chance. I'd love to hear your college selection stories.

Luke Skurman
CEO and Co-Founder
lukeskurman@collegeprowler.com

Welcome to College Prowler®

During the writing of College Prowler's guidebooks, we felt it was critical that our content was unbiased and unaffiliated with any college or university. We think it's important that our readers get honest information and a realistic impression of the student opinions on any campus—that's why if any aspect of a particular school is terrible, we (unlike a campus brochure) intend to publish it. While we do keep an eye out for the occasional extremist—the cheerleader or the cynic—we take pride in letting the students tell it like it is. We strive to create a book that's as representative as possible of each particular campus. Our books cover both the good and the bad, and whether the survey responses point to recurring trends or a variation in opinion, these sentiments are directly and proportionally expressed through our guides.

College Prowler guidebooks are in the hands of students throughout the entire process of their creation. Because you can't make student-written guides without the students, we have students at each campus who help write, randomly survey their peers, edit, layout, and perform accuracy checks on every book that we publish. From the very beginning, student writers gather the most up-to-date stats, facts, and inside information on their colleges. They fill each section with student quotes and summarize the findings in editorial reviews. In addition, each school receives a collection of letter grades (A through F) that reflect student opinion and help to represent contentment, prominence, or satisfaction for each of our 20 specific categories. Just as in grade school, the higher the mark the more content, more prominent, or more satisfied the students are with the particular category.

Once a book is written, additional students serve as editors and check for accuracy even more extensively. Our bounce-back team—a group of randomly selected students who have no involvement with the project—are asked to read over the material in order to help ensure that the book accurately expresses every aspect of the university and its students. This same process is applied to the 200-plus schools College Prowler currently covers. Each book is the result of endless student contributions, hundreds of pages of research and writing, and countless hours of hard work. All of this has led to the creation of a student information network that stretches across the nation to every school that we cover. It's no easy accomplishment, but it's the reason that our guides are such a great resource.

When reading our books and looking at our grades, keep in mind that every college is different and that the students who make up each school are not uniform—as a result, it is important to assess schools on a case-by-case basis. Because it's impossible to summarize an entire school with a single number or description, each book provides a dialogue, not a decision, that's made up of 20 different topics and hundreds of student quotes. In the end, we hope that this guide will serve as a valuable tool in your college selection process. Enjoy!

OMID GOHARI ◯ CHRISTINA KOSHZOW ◯ CHRIS MASON ◯ JOEY RAHIMI ◯ LUKE SKURMAN ◯

The College Prowler Team

VILLANOVA UNIVERSITY

Table of Contents

Introduction from the Author

I always enjoy telling people that I go to Villanova, because I never get the same response twice. Occasionally, I look at blank stares, then I follow up with where it's located, and then it's a quick "Oh yeah, I know that one," and the conversation moves on. But mostly what I get is a long list of friends that have gone here. Other times, it's the die-hard St. Joe's fans telling me that their team is better, but mostly, it's a shower of compliments about how hard it is to get in, and how academically competitive it is.

Villanova is a fairly hard school to get into—and it's only getting harder. When I speak to alumni, a common response is "I could never get in there now," and I have a feeling that in two or three years, I'll be saying the same thing. The administration works very hard to make the University better every year, and it shows. There is always some sort of construction going on—whether it's the older buildings being updated or new ones being built, Villanova is obviously growing. Even with class sizes remaining roughly the same, the students in them are getting smarter and more active. The name and reputation of Villanova carries weight, and in the Northeast, someone almost always knows someone else who went to Villanova. To me, it is only a matter of time before Villanova leaves its regional ranking of number one and becomes a nationally ranked university.

Villanova is a school built with tradition, held together with a strong sense of community, and filled with an ever-intellectual student body that constantly gives back to the less fortunate. It's been said that the average Villanova student studies five days a week, parties one day a week, and on the last day tries to save the world. Granted, this is probably not the case for everyone, but it does say something about the school. While no college is without parties, students here are, on the whole, focused and contributing to the academic prestige of the campus. Not only do the students here work hard for their grades, but an overwhelming amount spend a lot of their free time going into inner-city Philadelphia to work in soup kitchens, tutor in after-school programs, and volunteer for the annual Special Olympics of Pennsylvania held every year at Villanova.

By now, if you're still reading this, you obviously have some interest in the school. Whether you are familiar with the level of academics and professionalism the school provides, or if you just feel like Villanova has what you want, read on. Remember, going to college will be one of the hardest and most rewarding decisions you will ever make in your whole life. This book gives you every aspect of Villanova, the good and the bad; the rest is up to you. And hopefully, when all is said and done, you'll have a good idea if you want to make Villanova your home away from home for the best four years of your life.

Sean Wright, Author
Villanova University

By the Numbers

General Information

Villanova University
800 Lancaster Ave.
Villanova, PA 19085

Control:
Private

Academic Calendar:
Semester

Religious Affiliation:
Roman Catholic

Founded:
1842

Web Site:
www.villanova.edu

Main Phone:
(610) 519-6000

Student Body

Full-Time Undergraduates:
6,673

Part-Time Undergraduates:
677

Total Male Undergraduates:
3,607

Total Female Undergraduates:
3,743

Admissions

Overall Acceptance Rate:
42%

Early Decision Acceptance Rate:
Not offered

Early Action Acceptance Rate:
N/A

Regular Acceptance Rate:
42%

Total Applicants:
13,760

Total Acceptances:
5,718

Freshman Enrollment:
1,604

Yield (% of admitted students who actually enroll):
28%

Early Action Deadline:
November 1

Early Action Notification:
December 20

Regular Decision Deadline:
December 15 (priority)
January 7 (regular)

Regular Decision Notification:
April 1

Must-Reply-By Date:
May 1

Applicants Placed on Waiting List:
4,817

Applicants Accepting a Place on Waiting List:
2,077

Applicants Enrolled from Waiting List:
210

Transfer Applications Received:
565

Transfer Applications Accepted:
227

Transfer Students Enrolled:
133

Transfer Application Acceptance Rate:
40%

SAT I or ACT Required?
Yes, either

SAT I Range (25th–75th Percentile):
1190–1380

SAT I Verbal Range (25th–75th Percentile):
580–680

SAT I Math Range (25th–75th Percentile):
610–700

ACT Composite Range (25th–75th Percentile):
27–31

Top 10% of High School Class:
54%

Freshman Retention Rate:
94%

Common Application Accepted?
Yes

Supplemental Forms?
Required

➜

Application Fee:
$70

Admissions Phone:
(610) 519-4000

Admissions E-Mail:
gotovu@Villanova.edu

Admissions Web Site:
www.villanova.edu/enroll/admission

Financial Information

Full-Time Tuition:
$31,643

Room and Board:
$9,810

Books and Supplies:
$1,050

Average Need-Based Financial Aid Package (including loans, work-study, grants, and other sources):
$23,433

Students Who Applied for Financial Aid:
65%

Applicants Who Received Aid:
73%

Financial Aid Forms Deadline:
February 7

Financial Aid Phone:
(610) 519-4010

Financial Aid E-Mail:
finaid@villanova.edu

Financial Aid Web Site:
www.villanova.edu/enroll/finaid

Academics

The Lowdown On... Academics

Degrees Awarded:

Associate

Bachelor's

Post-bachelor's certificate

Master's

Post-master's certificate

Doctorate

First professional

Most Popular Majors:

34.8% Business/marketing

10.5% Social sciences

9.6% Engineering

8.9% Health sciences

7.4% Communications

Undergraduate Schools:

College of Engineering

College of Liberal Arts and Sciences

College of Nursing

Villanova School Business

Full-Time Faculty:
570

Faculty with Terminal Degree:
89%

Student-to-Faculty Ratio:
14:1

Average Course Load:
Five courses

Class Sizes:
Fewer than 20 Students: 42%
20 to 49 Students: 53%
50 or More Students: 5%

Graduation Rates:
Four-Year: 82%
Five-Year: 87%
Six-Year: 85%

Special Degree Options

Combined degree programs, accelerated program, double major, minor, independent study, study abroad, teacher certificates, undergraduate research projects

AP Test Score Requirements

Possible credit for scores of 3, 4 or 5

IB Test Score Requirements

Possible credit based on individual colleges

Best Places to Study

CEER, Connelly Center, Library

Sample Academic Clubs

Academic Competition Club, the Consumer Interest and Purchasing Club, the Marketing Society, National Society of Collegiate Scholars, the Villanova Entrepreneurial Society

Did You Know?

Do you want to get involved? One of the best ways to get involved at Villanova is the Special Olympics. It has **hosted Pennsylvania's Special Olympics for 16 consecutive years**. Over 2,000 students help volunteer for a weekend of fun, food, and unforgettable memories.

Don't feel like getting out of bed? Villanova now **offers a few of its courses online**. Villanova also provides space for your very own Web site.

Enjoy discussing current events within the context of history, philosophy, and theology? Villanova **requires a year long core humanities class** for all freshmen. Combining academics with Augustinian tradition, the core program covers a wide range of topics, and it gives you a feel for courses that are traditionally restricted to college, such as philosophy and theology.

Who doesn't like a good old parade? Every September, to celebrate St. Thomas of Villanova, the **University closes early for an afternoon of reflection, a parade, and good times**. Traveling across campus, the administration leads a parade that ends at Sheehan Beach, where you can chow down on some free barbeque food or just meet some new people.

Students Speak Out On... Academics

"Most of my teachers have been relatively interesting. My most boring classes are my lecture classes. Overall, I have been happy with my teachers."

"Without a doubt, **Villanova's teachers are the University's best asset**. The professors are famous for their availability through e-mail and office hours. No one fails at Villanova because the professor wasn't available to help. The core humanities seminar, required for all freshmen, is absolutely enthralling, combining aspects of history and philosophy, and every professor approaches the curriculum in different, yet engaging, ways."

"Good teachers are a rarity. They are stale, forced, and required; the bottom line is **no one is that excited to be there or to do well**."

"The teachers at Villanova are open, approachable, and genuinely concerned for their students' well-being and intellectual stimulation. **I find my classes interesting**."

"I had a wide range of good and bad teachers. Some of the **teachers would help me excessively, because that is how much they care about their students**. I had a calculus teacher that I ate dinner with, and I talk over Instant Messenger with him almost every day. Of course, I had some teachers who did not care about helping their students, and most students would just not care about them either."

"The teachers I have had thus far are a mix. Some are wonderful, some are horrendous. Overall, **the staff at Villanova is very intelligent**. Often, what makes a teacher bad is his teaching style, not his lack of knowledge. As a student, you need to learn to be flexible with learning techniques and find what works for you. The classes offered at Villanova are interesting. At times, the core curriculum can seem overwhelming, but the well-rounded knowledge you walk away with is definitely worth it. What is fun about Villanova's scheduling is you can take interesting classes that work to fulfill requirements."

"The teachers at Villanova are incredibly helpful. I have not had any that hasn't been fully interested in making all of their students succeed. They often give out their home phone numbers, and they encourage students to visit them during office hours or be in touch through e-mail at any time. As a political science major, I've found that all of my **professors have had hands-on world experience**. All of them not only teach brilliantly in their area of expertise, but they've been in the real world gaining experience in these areas."

"All my teachers are great, and they definitely can convey the new material to students really well. The **teachers are also very easy to access outside of class** through their office hours, and in fact, they encourage you to drop by either for a simple question or the most complex. Being in commerce and finance, all the classes I have found are very interesting, as they show me different aspects of the business world."

"All **Villanova professors are very available outside of class**. Most are eager to teach and want to see their students succeed."

"The teachers are generally very personable and caring, which in turn makes class enjoyable for me. There are, however, **some teachers that are very boring** who merely lecture. I find those classes very boring."

The College Prowler Take On... Academics

If there is one thing to be said about Villanova, it is that you will walk away with a solid education for a lifetime. The school attempts to provide each student with the best education, which is reflected through the dedication and knowledge of professors every time you enter the classroom. Granted, there are a few bad apples that have very little ambition to teach you anything. But these professors are a rarity. Every professor is subject to a survey on the quality of their teaching, and Student Government provides an online forum to discuss teachers freely.

Another added benefit is that there are no TAs teaching classes. While this might not seem like much, there is nothing worse than seeing TAs only a few years older than you trying to teach you material they just learned a few years ago themselves. This allows professors to get better acquainted with each student, and this also gives students the most knowledgeable person teaching. Plus, with the small class size, developing a positive working relationship with your professors is very easy and can be very helpful come test time. Overall, Villanova does a good job providing its students with competent professors who have a passion to be there and who are always willing to learn more or go beyond the books to help.

B+

The College Prowler® Grade on

Academics: B+

A high Academics grade generally indicates that professors are knowledgeable, accessible, and genuinely interested in their students' welfare. Other determining factors include class size, how well professors communicate, and whether or not classes are engaging.

Local Atmosphere

The Lowdown On... Local Atmosphere

Region:
Northeast

City, State:
Villanova, PA

Setting:
Suburb of Philadelphia

Distance from Philadelphia:
25 minutes

Distance from New York City:
2.5 hours

Points of Interest:
The Curtis Institute
Fairmount Park
Independence Hall
Independence Square
The Liberty Bell
Philadelphia Museum of Art
Valley Forge

Movie Theaters:

Bryn Mawr
824 Lancaster Ave., Bryn Mawr
(610) 520-7373

Clearview's Anthony Wayne
109 W. Lancaster Ave., Wayne
(610) 225-0980

UA King of Prussia Stadium 16
300 Goddard Blvd.
King of Prussia
(800) 326-3264

Shopping Malls:

Cherry Hill Mall
King of Prussia Mall
Market Place East
South Street

Major Sports Teams:

Eagles (football)
Flyers (hockey)
Phillies (baseball)
Sixers (basketball)

City Web Sites

www.phila.gov
www.philly.com
www.philadelphia.com
www.onebigcampus.com

Did You Know?

5 Fun Facts about Philadelphia:

- Philly has a long and interesting past. Founded in 1682, the city brims with its own history, culture, and atmosphere distinct to Philadelphia. As the **birthplace of American democracy**, Philly boasts Independence Hall, where patriots signed both the Declaration of Independence and the U.S. Constitution.
- With **nearly 50 major universities and colleges** in and around Philly, you never get tired of seeing the same old people, and the rivalries are for more than school pride.
- **Philadelphia's silver screen hero, Rocky Balboa** (Sylvester Stallone), trained and filmed in South Philly's Italian neighborhood and hit the bags in North Philly's Blue Horizon Boxing Club. Other movies filmed here are *The Sixth Sense*, *Fallen*, *Twelve Monkeys*, *Trading Spaces*, and *Blow Out* to name a few.
- Every New Year's Day, native **Philadelphians celebrate Mummermania, something resembling Mardi Gras** without the excuse of Lent. Having survived medieval folklore, court orders, and strict Puritan regulations, it still is celebrated in its entire historic splendor without much change from decades ago. A must see if you are in the city.
- The modern **Uilleann, a traditional Irish instrument** that is in the same family as the bagpipe, was ironically not developed in Ireland, but rather Philadelphia.

Famous People from Philadelphia:

Edmund Bacon
Kevin Bacon
Bill Cosby
Brian de Palma
W.C. Fields
Benjamin Franklin
Grace Kelly
Jack Kelly
M. Night Shyamalan
Will Smith

→

Local Slang:

Blue Route – I-476

The Mainline – Lancaster Ave., which can take you directly in and out of the city

Whiz-wit – requesting Cheese-Whiz with onions on your Philly cheesesteak

Whiz-witout – requesting Cheese-Whiz without onions on your Philly cheesesteak

Yo – a greeting like hello, rumored to have been popularized after the filming of Rocky

Students Speak Out On...
Local Atmosphere

"Philly is a good place to go to get out of the bubble. The town Villanova is in is suburbia in a nutshell. It's easy to get around if you have a car."

"Nearby **Philadelphia is brimming with possibilities**. During my first semester at Villanova, I saw four concerts, went to the Museum of Fine Arts, watched Villanova basketball at the storied Palestra, and partied at U Penn's frat row."

"The actual town of **Villanova is very residential, and there is not much to do**. It is a very nice area, though. Surrounding towns like Bryn Mawr, Ardmore, and Wayne have some nice restaurants and stores. There are no places I would stay away from in this area."

"The **towns immediately surrounding Villanova are unfriendly to students**. Bryn Mawr, which is minutes down Lancaster Avenue and home to Bryn Mawr University, is a bit friendlier. Bars and restaurants cater to students a bit more."

"Villanova is an upper-middle-class town without much fear of crime. **There are many universities in the area** to visit. You can always visit Philly, but there are parts of Philly you should stay away from."

"The town is okay. Being a city girl, it's hard not being able to walk out and hail a cab, but **there are cute little places to go if you have a car**."

"The Mainline is a very classy neighborhood, one that can easily give off the air of being snooty. But at the same time, it does offer **lots of nice shops, friendly cafés and restaurants**, and lots more. There are universities found up and down Lancaster Avenue, and even more right in Philadelphia. Villanova has a nice balance of a young college community right in the middle of a pleasant neighborhood setting."

"The **Mainline in Pennsylvania is truly a beautiful place**. Nestled 15 miles outside Philadelphia, it provides all the comfort, safety, and beauty of the suburbs, with the nightlife, culture, and fun of a nearby city. The surrounding towns of Bryn Mawr and Wayne are very close-knit communities and provide all the functions and services of any suburban area. There are several universities on the Mainline: Haverford, Eastern, Bryn Mawr, and Cabrini."

"I really like the surrounding area. There are **about six or seven colleges if you drive down one road**, but I barely ever leave campus, unless it's to go to the mall or something. I would recommend every place around here that I've been to."

"Villanova is set in a pretty much suburban atmosphere, but with close proximity to the city. There are a ton of smaller universities along the Mainline, but there is also a bunch in Philly that provide opportunities to hang out at other colleges. There really is not much to stay away from, but you definitely have to go to various parts of Philly. **South Street, the Linc, and downtown Philly are definitely places to frequent**."

"The town is great. It's a township comprised of several small towns, all of which possess a small-town feel. Since it's an upscale neighborhood, **there really is nothing to steer away from**, but plenty to check out, especially if you decide to go into the city."

The College Prowler Take On...
Local Atmosphere

Although Philadelphia is a good time for any college student—whether you like to party on the weekends or grab a cup of coffee and tour various art museums—as an underclassman, you are often restricted to areas closer to the campus. The surrounding towns vary in how they treat college students, but none represent a true college atmosphere. Don't let that stop you from having a good time, though. For six bucks and a short train ride, you can land yourself almost anywhere in the greater Philly area. Your best bet would be South Street, dubbed by many as the "hippest street in America," as it is a wealth of entertainment and Philly culture. Whether you're up for a night of clubbing, savoring Philly's cheesesteak rivals, or feasting on Jamaican jerky, South Street has endless opportunities for those restricted to mass transit.

If the bustle of city life is not your thing, Villanova's suburban communities also have a good deal to offer. Almost every town up and down the Mainline has a quaint small-town feel, with higher-end stores and restaurants. The closer you get to the city, the more likely you are to get a bigger bang for your buck. Because there is so much to do, it is difficult for students without cars to rely on mass transit to tap into all the activities out there.

B-

The College Prowler® Grade on

Local Atmosphere: B-

A high Local Atmosphere grade indicates that the area surrounding campus is safe and scenic. Other factors include nearby attractions, proximity to other schools, and the town's attitude toward students.

Safety & Security

The Lowdown On...
Safety & Security

Security Office:
Department of Public Safety
Farrell Hall
800 E. Lancaster Ave.
(610) 519-6979
(610) 519-4444 (emergencies)
publicsafety.villanova.edu

Number of VU Police:
76

Safety Services:
Campus escorts
Investigative division
Rape Aggression Defense
Ride Along program
WildCat Shuttle

→

→

Health Center

Health Services Building, Third Floor

(610) 519-4070

www.villanova.edu/studentlife/healthcenter

Hours: Daily 24 hours during the academic year; Monday–Friday 8 a.m.–4 p.m. during the summer.

Health Services:

Allergy shots

Basic medical

Flu shots and immunizations

Travel medicine

Women's health

Did You Know?

?

You are in good hands with VEMS. VEMS is a completely **student-run emergency service**. Since its start in 1989, VEMS is the only college-run program to have and maintain its very own building. VEMS also received the College EMS Organization of the Year award in 2001.

Students Speak Out On...
Safety & Security

"Campus security is so ubiquitous that most students curse it. You'll never feel worried about being in danger, but you will be worried about getting in trouble."

"I have **never felt unsafe on the campus of Villanova**. I walk alone at night with no fears. The presence of Public Safety officers can be seen and felt, and there has never been a serious need for them, in my opinion."

"Security guards at Villanova do a **good job of protecting the campus**. I have no fears walking around campus late at night by myself. I never had to fear my roommate or any neighbors stealing my personal items, which made me feel secure at Villanova."

"I feel very safe on campus, but I think that is because I am comfortable here. **I don't think our campus has many security regulations** other than WildCards and campus safety officers."

The community surrounding Villanova is really the biggest reason that there is so much security on campus. It's a nice neighborhood where **everyone looks out for one another**. There are many residences and families living across the street, and this provides for a very neighborly feel on campus."

"**They are overprotective**, but I do admit, I feel safe going anywhere at 2 a.m."

"The University is incredibly safe with very few security incidents occurring each year. I feel completely comfortable walking from one end of campus to the other by myself at night, even though there are plenty of options if I didn't. There's a late-night shuttle service, plenty of emergency call-boxes, and Public Safety is constantly monitoring the grounds, particularly on weekends. Most **buildings have guards during the evening, and the doors are always locked** to prevent outside intruders."

"Villanova's campus is very safe. I have never felt nervous or uneasy about walking back to my dorm late at night after a long night at the library. Everything is well lit. **Public Safety can be considered to be too protective**, especially in the signing-in of friends."

"**Public Safety officers seem to be crawling everywhere**, whether this is for the good or the bad. I was at the girls' lacrosse game today, and there were three different event staff people and two Public Safety officers."

"**Villanova is so safe it's pathetic**. Security is everywhere, and the surrounding area is the safest environment imaginable."

"Security is always present on campus, and they are always available if there's a problem. **I always feel very safe while I'm walking** on campus alone or even late at night."

The College Prowler Take On...
Safety & Security

Any student you ask will say he or she feels very secure on campus. With a strong presence by Public Safety and a safe neighborhood nestled in a quiet suburban area, there is little to worry about. There are hardly ever incidents even worth mentioning, and when they do come up, such as a fight or major theft, Public Safety usually deals with them quickly. Outside of that, the security policies for entering and exiting buildings are fairly lax, although the freshman dorms on South Campus tend to be strict when trying to enter the building after visitation hours. Generally, though, with a quick show of the WildCard, there shouldn't be any problems. The most common things to be stolen are laptops, but even this only happens on occasion.

However, Public Safety does come down heavy on student drinking, and they have been known to ask students to see what's in duffel bags being carried around at night. For something like that, they are quick to fine you and take the disciplinary action the school requires, but for most other things, they tend not to have such a heavy hand. So while they are strict on underage drinking, they do keep a safe atmosphere around campus and allow students to be pretty much worry free walking around late at night.

A

The College Prowler® Grade on

Safety & Security: A

A high grade in Safety & Security means that students generally feel safe, campus police are visible, blue-light phones and escort services are readily available, and safety precautions are not overly necessary.

Computers

The Lowdown On... Computers

High-Speed Network?
Yes

Wireless Network?
Yes, in selected places

Number of Labs:
3

Number of Computers:
About 200

Operating Systems:
Mac OS, UNIX, Windows

Discounted Software

Villanova's UNIT Department has a special partnership with Dell, so any software and computer purchases through Dell are discounted, varying from product to product.

Free Software

Adobe Acrobat Reader, Adobe Acrobat Writer, Animation and 3D Design, Bryce 3D, Cool 3D, Corel Draw, Corel Photo House, Corel Presentations, Corel Quattro Pro, Corel WordPerfect 8, Graphic Design and Editors, Microsoft Access, Microsoft Binder, Microsoft Excel, Microsoft Outlook, Microsoft PowerPoint, Microsoft Word, Netscape Communicator, Illustrator 4.0, PageMaker 4.0, Photoshop 5.0, Paint Shop Pro, Art Z II, Unlead GIF Animator

24-Hour Labs

Mendel and Tolentine

Charge to Print?

No, all students have an annual print allowance; after that, black and white prints are 6 cents, and colors are 12 cents.

Students Speak Out On...
Computers

"You should definitely bring your own computer; however, there are several computer labs throughout campus that are accessible to students."

"We have **wireless networks in addition to the Internet hookups throughout campus**, which allow you to travel freely with your PC. The labs are never crowded, and there are many places around campus to print materials, as well."

"The network in my dorm is at least a little bit slower than the rest of campus, but it still is pretty fast. You should definitely **bring your own computer**, probably a laptop, so you can take it with you to the library or to class."

"I am a business major, so I had to get a Dell through the school. **The computer network is amazing here** at Villanova. Every time my computer broke down, the tech support team repaired it fast, and they were reliable. The wired and wireless connection is extremely fast. If you do not own a computer, there are still tons of places where you can find one available. I recommend bringing your own computer from home if you do not buy one through the school."

"The computer network is excellent. I love the computer labs, which can be crowded during the day, but I've never waited for more than a minute for a computer. Definitely **bring your own computer**, and do not buy one from the school, they rip students off. Your own computer is a great luxury, but by no means a necessity."

"Bringing your own computer is a nice luxury to have, but not having one is still manageable. **There are a sufficient amount of computers on campus**. They are spread out, which can pose a problem. If one lab is full, you need to walk to the library. If you find that full, you need to go to another building, and so on. You find computers most likely to be filled around midterms and finals, but that's not surprising."

"I would definitely bring your own computer, just for laziness reasons. Sometimes **you don't want to leave your room every time you want to check your e-mail**. I'm completely lost without my computer, and if my roommate didn't have one, it would be pure chaos. But, I think it's good to use the computer labs to print things, so you don't waste the ink or the paper."

"With my laptop, I never really need to use the computer labs, unless it is to go to the print center. The computer **labs are pretty easily accessible**, and they are not crowded. Bringing your own computer is definitely what needs to be done, though. I have not heard of any laptop thefts, so you should get a laptop if possible."

"**No one uses the computer labs**, so if you need to, you'll be fine. The network isn't that bad either. We get the occasional virus, or the Web site might be down for a couple of hours, but besides that, there's nothing to worry about."

"Villanova provides **many opportunities to keep up with the advancing high-tech age**. They offer many deals for purchasing your own laptop through the University if you do not already own a computer, and they have a fabulous computer support center that is always ready to answer questions and fix problems on a walk-in basis."

"The computer network is really great here. **Every dorm has Internet connections**, as do many of the classrooms, and several computer labs are available to students. I would, however, bring my own computer to Villanova for ease."

"You can bring your own computer, but you don't need it. And **you definitely don't need your own printer**, because there are many facilities on campus you can use for free printing."

The College Prowler Take On... Computers

Villanova's computer network is top-notch. Almost every single aspect of college life revolves around the computer, from homework to registering for classes; it's all done over the network. The network is fast, and every building has access to it. Everywhere you go, you'll find green and gray ports along the walls to plug in your laptop, and UNIT is in the final phases of converting every building to support wireless. However, if you're not using wireless and have a laptop, a word of caution—Villanova makes its own Internet cables, so if you have a cable from home, don't bring it. It's also really frustrating, sometimes, that only some buildings take green wires, while others only take gray. Your best bet is to go to UNIT before school starts and buy both, that way you are covered for every building.

Also, if you have your own computer, bring it. While there are computers all over campus with a relatively short wait, sometimes it's just nicer to have your own. There is a purchase program that is run through the school that allows for cheaper prices, but again, it's better to purchase your own. However, whether you have wireless, a regular laptop, desktop, or no computer at all, getting to a computer is never hard, and printing is always free.

B+

The College Prowler® Grade on

Computers: B+

A high grade in Computers designates that computer labs are available, the computer network is easily accessible, and the campus' computing technology is up-to-date.

Facilities

The Lowdown On... Facilities

Student Center:
Connelly Center

Athletic Center:
Jake Nevin Field House
The Pavilion

Libraries:
Falvey Memorial Library

Campus Size:
254 acres

Popular Places to Chill:
Connelly Center
Mendel Field
The Oreo
Second Story Quad
Sheehan Beach

What Is There to Do on Campus?

When you get tired of pushing papers and reading volumes of your least favorite intro class, take a break to see a movie at Connelly Center, play pool in St. Mary's or Connelly, hit the weights at Stanford or Farley, or rent a movie from Reel Divine, and take it easy.

Movie Theater on Campus?

Yes, Connelly Center

Bowling on Campus?

No

Bar on Campus?

No

Coffeehouse on Campus?

Yes, Holy Grounds in four locations

Favorite Things to Do

If you are ever bored, just head over to the Connelly Center. If you missed a movie in the theaters, Connelly's cinema will most likely be playing it just a few months later for free. During the day, there are always tons of people playing shuffleboard, foosball, pool, checking their e-mails, or just napping on the overstuffed couches in the cyber café. Some other fun things to do are checking out sporting events at the Pavilion and the stadium.

Students Speak Out On...
Facilities

"The facilities on campus are pretty nice, but the only problem with them is that all of the facilities close down very early. For example, there are no dining halls open after 10 p.m."

"**The student center, Connelly, is a great place** to hang out, get food, drink coffee, eat ice cream, play pool, watch movies, and attend many events. Every weekend, there are plenty of activities available for entertainment. There are always free movie showings of newly-released films, and there's always a program of some sort, like a battle of the bands, a comedian, or some type of live entertainment."

"There are **two weight rooms/workout facilities open that are free to students**, as well as several gyms and a pool. As with any school that thoroughly supports its athletic program, the varsity weight rooms far surpass the regular student used ones, but both are fully functional with plenty of equipment."

"The facilities are outstanding at Villanova. Perhaps the athletic and student facilities are not as great as some state schools, but the **facilities are amazing for the size of the University**. The student center has fast food made by the University and an ice cream store where people can use their meal plan. The movie theater is also a nice touch. The student center has some other rooms that are used for dances or meeting rooms. Overall, the facilities at Villanova are very nice!"

"The weight rooms, excluding the athletes only facility, could be nicer. There is a bevy of **basketball courts and open fields for pick-up games**. I loved playing intramural soccer on Jake Nevin Field. I love the computer labs. The library needs a ton of work. The Connelly Center is awesome."

"The major facilities that are lacking are the student gyms. There are two exercise rooms around campus. Both have machines and free weights, but neither is very impressive. The **gyms are often crowded**, have lines for machines, or broken ones. That is definitely one area that could stand some improvement."

"Yes, they are very nice. I got surgery on my torn ACL at the end of the summer, and I was a frequent visitor to physical therapy. The people were especially nice, and they gave you a lot of personal attention. The machines were great, new, and really helped my knee get better. I like the basketball court, although it could be bigger. The print center in Bartley could have more computers. I like the cyber lounge. Overall, I believe that **Villanova is a great campus with spectacular facilities**."

"All the facilities on campus are **very well maintained and kept up**. The athletic facilities for students are extremely lacking, but since this is a very hot topic on campus, hopefully some new facilities will be in sight soon."

"The **athletic facilities for non-varsity athletes need extreme renovation**. I use the gym at the bottom of Stanford. There are no elliptical machines, and students often have to wait for treadmills and Stairmasters at prime gym times. Also, there are no televisions, and the room itself is ugly and smelly. The computer labs get full at prime times, as well, but people go in and out quickly, so you rarely have to wait at all. The student center is very well kept."

"I've been told **the gyms need to be updated** and one added on Main. The computers are fine, depending on where you go; Mendel and Bartley have the best from what I know. The Connolly Center is great. It has a cinema, ice cream, and a dining area."

"Most of the **facilities on campus are very well-kept**, but I do think that the athletic facilities could use some renovation, especially the gyms on South and West campus."

"We have **nice facilities with good hours**, and they aren't too crowded even during 'busy' times."

"I think the most lacking facilities are athletics. The **student center is well equipped**, as are the computer labs."

The College Prowler Take On... Facilities

All roads lead to the Connelly Center. It is not only geographically in the middle of campus, it is also the social center, study center, and has arguably the best food on campus. It caters to the student's basic needs. One need that tends to be overlooked is the athletic facilities. Both West and South campus gyms often have broken equipment and long lines to use the machines that actually work. However, the athletic facilities are being updated to meet student needs. Something Villanova does have a lot of, though, are courts. Every dorm on campus is within a few minutes walk of tennis, volleyball, and basketball courts, and there is almost never a wait for a pick-up game.

Overall, the facilities on campus add to the feel of the school. The building that always gives postcard quality pictures is the church, the oldest building on campus. But even the newer buildings on campus revert to the older look with modern accommodations. However, no campus is complete without a few buildings that stick out like sore thumbs. Perched on top of a hill, CEER is a massive white concrete monster of a building that contrasts directly with Tolentine, one of the oldest buildings on campus. The only area that the University seems to overlook is the need for up-to-date athletic facilities.

B

The College Prowler® Grade on

Facilities: B

A high Facilities grade indicates that the campus is aesthetically pleasing and well-maintained; facilities are state-of-the-art, and libraries are exceptional. Other determining factors include the quality of both athletic and student centers and an abundance of things to do on campus.

Campus Dining

The Lowdown On...
Campus Dining

Meal Plan Average Cost:

$575–$2,360

Each meal plan includes a certain number of meals per week, meal points, and guest meals.

Freshman Meal Plan Requirement?

Yes

Places to Grab a Bite with Your Meal Plan:

Belle Aire Terrace

Food: Sandwiches, Asian

Location: Connelly Center

Hours: Monday–Thursday 8 a.m.–10 p.m., Friday 8 a.m.–9 p.m., Saturday 11 a.m.–9 p.m., Sunday 12 p.m.–10 p.m.; Grab and Go: Sunday–Thursday 10 a.m.–12 a.m.

→

The Corner Grille

Food: American

Location: Dougherty Hall

Hours: Monday–Thursday 10:45 a.m.–6:15 p.m., Friday 10:45 a.m.–2 p.m.

Donahue Court (The Spit)

Food: Buffet

Location: Donahue Hall

Hours: Monday–Friday 7:30 a.m.–10 a.m., 11:30 a.m.–2:30 p.m., 4:15 p.m.–7:45 p.m., Saturday–Sunday 10:30 a.m.–4 p.m., 4:15 p.m.–7:45 p.m.

Donohue Market

Food: Convenience store

Location: Donohue Court

Hours: Monday–Friday 10 a.m.–1 a.m., Saturday–Sunday 1 p.m.–1 a.m.

Dougherty Hall

Food: Buffet with salad bar

Location: Basement of Dougherty Hall

Hours: Monday–Friday 7:30 a.m.–10:30 a.m., 10:45 a.m.–2:30 p.m., 4:15 p.m.–7:15 p.m., Saturday–Sunday 7:30 a.m.–4 p.m., 4:15 p.m.–7:15 p.m.

The Exchange

Food: Deli, hot entrees

Location: Bartley Hall

Hours: Monday–Thursday 8 a.m.–8:15 p.m.,

(The Exchange, continued)

Friday 8 a.m–2:30 p.m., Saturday 8 a.m.–2 p.m.

Ice Cream Shoppe

Food: Ice cream, milkshakes, frozen yogurt

Location: Connolly Center

Hours: Monday–Friday 12 p.m.–10 p.m., Saturday–Sunday 1 p.m.–10 p.m.

The Italian Kitchen

Food: Italian

Location: Dougherty Hall

Hours: Monday–Thursday 10:45 a.m.–7:30 p.m., Friday 10:45 a.m.–7 p.m.

Holy Grounds

Food: Coffee, espresso, cappuccino, sandwiches, baked goods

Locations: 4

Hours: CEER: Monday–Thursday 8 a.m.–8 p.m., Friday 8 a.m.–2:30 p.m., Saturday 8 a.m.–2 p.m.

Connelly Center: Monday–Thursday 8 a.m.–11 p.m., Friday 8 a.m.–10 p.m., Saturday 10 a.m.–10 p.m., Sunday 11 a.m.–11 p.m.

The Exchange: Monday–Thursday 8 a.m.–11 p.m., Friday 8 a.m.–4:15 p.m.

Falvey Library: Monday–Thursday 8 a.m.–10 p.m., Friday 8 a.m.–4 p.m., Sunday 11 a.m.–10 p.m.

The Law School Café

Food: Grab 'n go sandwiches, salads, bakery

Location: Garey Hall

Hours: Monday–Thursday 8 a.m.–7 p.m., Friday 8 a.m.–2 p.m.

Second Storey

Food: Convenience store

Location: St. Mary's Hall

Hours: Monday–Friday 9 a.m.–2 a.m., Saturday–Sunday 12 p.m.–2 a.m.

St. Augustine Café

Food: Sandwiches, soups, salads, hot entrees

Location: Liberal Arts Center

Hours: Monday–Friday 8 a.m.–2 p.m.

St. Mary's Hall

Food: Buffet with salad bar

Location: St. Mary's Hall

Hours: Monday–Friday 7:30 a.m.–10:30 a.m., 10:45 a.m.–2 p.m., 4:15 p.m.–7:15 p.m., Saturday–Sunday 10:30 a.m.–4 p.m., 4:15 p.m.–7:15 p.m.

Student Favorites:

Belle Aire Terrace

The Corner Grille

The Italian Kitchen

Off-Campus Places to Use Your Meal Plan:

None

24-Hour On-Campus Dining?

None

Other Options

While there are no places off campus that accept a meal plan, many take the WildCard, only they deduct from the debit account. The majority of fast food places and restaurants in the area do this, and they are very friendly to students.

Did You Know?

Villanova's Dining Services won the 2004 **Restaurants and Institutions Ivy Award**, one of the highest awards for the food service industry.

Students Speak Out On... Campus Dining

"The food on campus is okay; it is nothing special. My favorite spot to go is Second Storey for either a great sandwich or decent hot foods."

"**The food is sub-par at times**, and it's really hit or miss. The dining halls are okay, although I prefer the coffee places and the cyber lounge."

"Campus food is good—once you get used to it. Everyone just has to realize nothing beats home cooking. Some **good spots on campus are Donahue Court (a.ka the Spit) and Belle Air Terrace** in the Connelly Center. The dining halls are good enough. Watch out that you don't eat excessive amounts of junk food, because you will gain the Freshman 15."

"Villanova offers a wide range of dining services. There are **three traditional dining halls**, and while, like all college students, we grumble about the quality, they are actually pretty good. There are a number of coffee places, called 'Holy Grounds,' which offer pretty good coffee."

"**Food on campus is good**. Granted, it is still college food, but it is good. There's also a pretty good selection. There are a lot of different places to eat, so you can switch it up on a daily basis. The Italian Kitchen and the Corner Grille are two great places for lunch. You can get fresh sandwiches or Philly cheesesteaks, as well as pasta or hamburgers."

"I have heard of worse food on other campuses. We can complain, but **it just makes food at home taste that much better**."

"**The food is reasonable**. I eat at the main dining halls most of the time, just because they have the most selection, and I can get as much food as I want to eat that night. Belle Air has really good wraps and sandwiches. I am a fan of the low-fat Wawa chocolate milk they have in the dining halls."

"The food on campus is definitely good. There are a ton of different places to eat. Generally, **freshmen eat at the Spit or Donahue Hall**, which offers a ton of different food and is the only spot on South Campus to eat. On Main Campus, some hot spots are the Italian Kitchen and the Connelly Center. The Exchange in Bartley's is my personal favorite, as far as sandwiches and wraps go, though."

"**The mac and cheese at Second Storey is the best food on campus**. You can get it in St. Mary's from 10:30 a.m. to 2 a.m. every day of the week. I get it almost every day; I'm a big supporter of the mac and cheese. For breakfast, it is usually waffles, pancakes, or something to that effect with a piece of cantaloupe. There is much better food here than there is in other colleges."

"**People tend to like the Spit the best**. The food is alright. Villanova puts a lot of money into making it good, and every month, they have some specialty night with interesting ethnic food."

"The **food is typical college dining hall food**, but you get used to it. Some great spots to know would be Second Storey and the Connelly Center, since they both offer diverse foods."

"All of the dining halls provide a wide array of options for what to eat. **The Spit, Dougherty, and St. Mary's are all buffet-style unlimited dining**. The Belle Aire Terrace, the Italian Kitchen and the Corner Grill have take-out options that are based on how much food you get. There are two convenience markets on campus for a quick snack, and all of these places accept a meal plan. In addition, there are several coffee shops called Holy Grounds and an ice cream shop."

"I like the Italian Kitchen the most, because of the variety of sandwiches I can get. Also, there are **always salads available to go**. I wish that there weren't the same things everyday—burgers, chicken wings, and so on, but I expected that."

"The **food on campus is not bad**. I usually eat at the Connolly Center or at the Italian Kitchen."

The College Prowler Take On... Campus Dining

College food, no matter where you go, is never even close to a home-cooked meal. That's always one of the reasons going home on breaks is that much better. That aside, Villanova has a decent selection of pretty edible food. All types of eating preferences are looked after, whether you are vegetarian, vegan, or have religious eating restrictions, dining services offers other options. Not to mention that if you are hungry, there are always the three cafeterias that have decent food—and as much as you can eat. Breakfast is always good, with a variety of eggs, sandwiches, omelets, pancakes, and fruit.

It also helps that there are plenty of food specialty places around campus. The only problem with these, though, is that they tend to close early for a college campus and leave you in a position to get takeout or snack on something in the room. Overall, Villanova has a good taste in what is served. While students like to complain, it's not all that bad.

B+

The College Prowler® Grade on

Campus Dining: B+

Our grade on Campus Dining addresses the quality of both school-owned dining halls and independent on-campus restaurants as well as the price, availability, and variety of food.

Off-Campus Dining

The Lowdown On... Off-Campus Dining

Restaurant Prowler: Popular Places to Eat!

Bertucci's Brick Oven Ristorante

Food: Italian, brick-oven pizza

761 Lancaster Ave., Bryn Mawr

(610) 519-1940

www.bertuccis.com

Cool Features: Tons of pizza toppings made in brick ovens

Price: $10–$20

(Bertucci's, continued)

Hours: Monday–Thursday 11 a.m.–10 p.m., Friday–Saturday 11 a.m.–11 p.m., Sunday 12 p.m.–10 p.m.

Campus Corner

Food: Pizza, sandwiches

829 Lancaster Ave., Villanova

(610) 527-3606

Cool Features: Late-night eats for those munchies

Price: $5–$10

→

(Campus Corner, continued)

Hours: Sunday–Thursday 11 a.m.–1 a.m., Friday–Saturday 11 a.m.–2 a.m.

The Cheesecake Factory

Food: American

570 Mall Blvd., King of Prussia

(610) 337-2200

www.thecheesecakefactory.com

Cool Features: Tons of cheesecakes and great food

Price: $10–$20

Hours: Daily 11 a.m.–2 a.m.

China Garden

Food: Chinese

906 Conestoga Rd., Bryn Mawr

(610) 525-4210

Cool Features: Take-out and delivery available

Price: $10–$15

Hours: Monday–Thursday 11 a.m.–11 p.m., Friday–Saturday 11 a.m.–11:30 p.m., Sunday 12 p.m.–11 p.m.

Christopher's

Food: American, bar

108 N. Wayne St., Wayne

(610) 687-6558

Cool Features: Great food, neighborhood bar

Price: $10–$15

Hours: Monday–Saturday 11 a.m.–1 a.m., Sunday 11 a.m.–2 a.m.

Fellini's Cafe

Food: Italian

31 E. Lancaster Ave., Ardmore

(610) 642-9009

Price: $15–$20

Hours: Sunday–Thursday 11 a.m.–9:30 p.m., Friday–Saturday 11 a.m.–10 p.m.

Garrett Hill Pizza

Food: Pizza, Italian

910 Conestoga Rd., Bryn Mawr

(610) 525-8842

Price: $8–$10

Hours: Monday–Thursday 10:30 a.m.–12 a.m., Friday–Saturday 10:30 a.m.–1 a.m., Sunday 10:30 a.m.–12 a.m.

Geno's Steaks

Food: Cheesesteaks, deli

1219 S. 9th St., Philadelphia

(215) 389-0659

www.genosteaks.com

Cool Features: Home of the original cheesesteak

Price: $4–$7

Hours: Daily 24 hours

Great Harvest Bread Co.

Food: Bakery, bread

128 E. Lancaster Ave., Wayne

(610) 975-0200

www.greatharvest.com

Cool Features: Free samples of any bread of the day

Price: $5–$10

(Great Harvest, continued)

Hours: Tuesday–Saturday
5 a.m.–6:30 p.m.,
Sunday 8 a.m.–5 p.m.

Grog Restaurant & Bar

Food: Bar, American

863 W. Lancaster Ave.
Bryn Mawr

(610) 527-5870

Price: $10–$15

Cool Features: Comfortable atmosphere, great bar food

Hours: Monday–Thursday
11 a.m.–10 p.m.,
Friday 12 p.m.–11 p.m.,
Saturday 12 p.m.–10 p.m.,
Sunday 12 p.m.–9 p.m.

Gullifty's Pizza Grille & Bar

Food: American, Italian

1149 Lancaster Ave. Rosemont

(610) 525-1851

www.gulliftys.com

Cool Features: Weekly karaoke and family nights

Price: $10–$20

Hours: Sunday–Tuesday
11 a.m.–11 p.m.,
Wednesday 11 a.m.–2 a.m.,
Thursday 11 a.m.–1 a.m.,
Friday–Saturday 11 a.m.–2 a.m.

Hunan Garden

Food: Chinese

2212 West Chester Pike
Broomall

(610) 356-7497

(Hunan Garden, continued)

Cool Features: Take-out and delivery available

Price: $10–$12

Hours: Daily 10:30 a.m.–10 p.m.

Jim's Steaks

Food: Cheesesteaks, deli

400 South St., Philadelphia

(215) 928-1911

www.jimssteaks.com

Cool Features: They ship steaks in the U.S. overnight

Price: $5–$10

Hours: Sunday–Thursday
10 a.m.–1 a.m., Friday–
Saturday 10 a.m.–3 a.m.

John Harvard's Brew House

Food: American

629 W. Lancaster Ave., Wayne

(610) 687-6565

www.johnharvards.com

Cool Features: Brew all of their own beers and seasonal brews

Price: $5–$18

Hours: Monday–Thursday
11:30 a.m.–12:30 a.m., Friday–
Saturday 11:30 a.m.–1 a.m.,
Sunday 11:30 a.m.–12 a.m.

Marita's Cantina

Food: Southwest

610 W. Lancaster Ave.
Bryn Mawr

(610) 527-8989

Cool Features: Fun dishes and Mexican drinks

(Marita's Cantina, continued)

Price: $12–$15

Hours: Sunday–Thursday 11:30 a.m.–10 p.m., Friday–Saturday 11:30 a.m.–10:30 p.m.

Mikado Japanese Restaurant

Food: Japanese

66 E. Lancaster Ave., Ardmore

(610) 645-5592

Cool Features: Long sushi bar, private party rooms

Price: $10–$15

Hours: Monday–Thursday 12 p.m.–2:45 p.m., 5 p.m.–9:45 p.m., Friday–Saturday 12 p.m.–2:45 p.m., 5 p.m.–10:15 p.m., Sunday 4 p.m.–9:15 p.m.

Minella's Mainline Diner

Food: American

320 W. Lancaster Ave., Wayne

(610) 687-1575

Cool Features: After a night of partying, chill out for some late-night snacks

Price: $5–$10

Hours: Daily 24 hours

The New Tavern Restaurant and Bar

Food: American

261 Montgomery Ave. Bala Cynwyd

(610) 667-9100

www.thetavernrestaurant.com

Cool Features: Daily specials, outdoor terrace

(New Tavern, continued)

Price: $5–$28

Hours: Monday–Thursday 11:30 a.m.–3 p.m., 5 p.m.–10 p.m., Friday–Saturday 11:30 a.m.–3 p.m., 5 p.m.–10:30 p.m.

Pat's King of Steaks

Food: Cheesesteaks, deli

1237 E. Passyunk Ave. Philadelphia

(215) 468-1546

www.patskingofsteaks.com

Cool Features: Celebrities get their cheesesteaks here

Price: $5–$8

Hours: Daily 24 hours

Peace A Pizza

Food: Pizza

4 Station Rd., Ardmore

(610) 896-4488

Price: $5–$10

Hours: Sunday–Thursday 11 a.m.–9 p.m., Friday–Saturday 11 a.m.–10 p.m.

Peace A Pizza

1125 W. Lancaster Ave. Rosemont

(610) 581-7010

www.peacepizza.com

Cool Features: Not your traditional pizza toppings

Price: $3–$10

Hours: Sunday–Thursday 11 a.m.–10 p.m., Friday–Saturday 11 a.m.–11 p.m.

The Point
Food: Coffeehouse
117 W. Wayne Ave., Wayne
(866) 468-7619
www.pointentertainment.com
Cool Features: Live music, open mic nights
Price: $5–$10
Hours: Monday–Thursday 9 a.m.–11 p.m., Friday–Saturday 9 a.m.–12 a.m., Sunday 11 a.m.–10 p.m.

Thai Peppers
Food: Thai
64 E. Lancaster Ave., Ardmore
(610) 642-5951
OR
372 W. Lancaster Ave., Wayne
(610) 688-5853
Cool Features: Healthy dishes, take-out available
Price: $10–$20
Hours: Ardmore: Daily 11:30 a.m.–3 p.m., 5 p.m.–10 p.m.
Wayne: Monday–Thursday 11:30 a.m.–3 p.m., 5 p.m.–10 p.m., Friday–Saturday 11:30 a.m.–3 p.m., 5 p.m.–10:30 p.m., Sunday 4 p.m.–9:30 p.m.

Vinny Testa's
Food: Italian
260 E. Lancaster Ave. Wynnewood
(610) 645-5400
www.vinnytestas.com
Cool Features: Family-style dinners, made from scratch
Price: $6–$25
Hours: Monday–Thursday 11:30 a.m.–10 p.m., Friday–Saturday 11:30 a.m.–11 p.m., Sunday 12 p.m.–10 p.m.

The Wild Onion
Food: Bar, American
900 Conestoga Rd., Rosemont
(610) 527-4826
www.thewildonion.com
Cool Features: Daily specials and theme nights
Price: $10–$15
Hours: Monday–Saturday 11:30 a.m.–2 a.m., Sunday 12 p.m.–2 a.m.

Wingers
Food: Chicken, wings
819 E. Lancaster Ave., Villanova
(610) 519-0300
Price: $8–$10
Hours: Sunday–Thursday 11 a.m.–1 a.m., Friday–Saturday 11 a.m.–2:30 a.m.

Other Places to Check Out:

Chili's

Citron

Cosi

Hope's Cookie's
Morton's

Student Favorites:

Campus Corner

Geno's Steaks

The Grog

Jim's Steaks

Minella's Mainline Diner

Pat's King of Steaks

Wingers

Grocery Stores:

Acme Markets, Inc.

600 W. Lancaster Ave.
Bryn Mawr

(610) 520-0280

Genuardi's Family Market

550 E. Lancaster Ave.
St. David's

(610) 989-0781

24-Hour Dining:

Thai Peppers

Geno's Steaks

Minella's Mainline Diner

Pat's King of Steaks

Late-Night Snacking:

Campus Corner

Wingers

Best Breakfast:

Minella's Mainline Diner

Best Chinese:

China Garden

Best Healthy:

Mikado Japanese Restaurant

The Point

Best Pizza:

Campus Corner

Peace A Pizza

Best Wings:

Wingers

Best Place to Take Your Parents:

Bertucci's Brick Oven Ristorante

The Cheesecake Factory

Gullifty's Pizza Grille & Bar

John Harvard's Brew House

Vinny Testa's

Students Speak Out On...
Off-Campus Dining

"I love the places that take WildCard for delivery. I have never gotten anything at Campus Corner that I did not like."

"My **favorite spot is John Harvard's Brew House**—a friendly college atmosphere with great burgers and home-brewed beers. There are many great chains as well, including Chili's, Bertucci's, and Cheesecake Factory, and an array of choices at the King of Prussia Mall only 15 minutes away."

"There are so many great restaurants in Philadelphia. Basically, **almost every major chain restaurant and some local restaurants are in Philly**. Anything you are hungry for, Philly will have it, from expensive restaurants like Morton's steakhouse, to cheap fast food chains, local Philly cheesesteak places, and good Italian restaurants."

"Off-campus restaurants are great. **Mikado is supreme for sushi**. Citron is also good. Wingers is good for simple grilled foods, and the chicken in pita is the best. Philly has great places as well."

"The Mainline offers plenty of great restaurants. Try **Fellini's for great Mediterranean cuisine** at reasonable prices. The ambience and service is incredible, so you shouldn't be surprised by a long wait sometimes. (It is BYOB, be careful.)"

"The best place to order food from is Campus Corner. The wings and the garlic bread with cheese are to die for. If you're looking to go out, you can walk right over, it's just on the corner of campus. If you want a sit down restaurant, **Lancaster Avenue has tons of places** to go. There are chain restaurants like Berrtucci's or John Harvard's, or you can find an intimate café or Italian restaurant. Do keep in mind, though, that it is the Mainline, so dinner can be expensive."

"Restaurants off campus are great. **John Harvard's, Thai Pepper, Peace A Pizza, Hope's Cookies, Gullifty's**, and others are all good stuff. Plus, Philly provides some good eating areas."

"There are lots of great restaurants right down the road from Villanova. **A few good spots to go would be Peace A Pizza, Marita's Cantina, and the Thai Pepper**. A little bit further from campus, there is the King of Prussia Mall, which has some fantastic restaurants, and of course, you can always go into Philly for a night out at some great places."

"Restaurants off campus are really great. **Some popular student spots include Cosi, John Harvard's**, Bertucci's, Christopher's, and Gullifty's."

"**It's very easy to get off campus** if you choose. There are two train stations on campus that take you to different parts of the surrounding areas. So, if you choose to have a meal off campus, it's easy to get to."

"The **restaurants off campus are very good**. At most of the restaurants you can get a good meal for a decent price."

The College Prowler Take On...
Off-Campus Dining

One of the best aspects of the Greater Philadelphia area is the range of good food available to almost anyone, from the college student to a family going out to celebrate—Philly has it all. Within the immediate towns of Villanova, you can get Thai, Chinese, American, Italian, and so on, all for an affordable price. A good idea for any student is to sample some of the ethnic cuisine just a stone's throw from the school. Most of the places are pretty cheap and like college kids! While pizza and french fries usually end up being the staple foods for most students, you should also be willing to diversify and try some of the other foods that Philly has to offer, namely its pretzels and the must-have Philly cheesesteak. While most cities have a "best pizza" restaurant, in Philly it's all about who has the best cheesesteak, and it's more than a matter of pride. At least once, every student should head down to South Street and try Jim's, Pat's, and Geno's.

The Greater Philly area has been argued for by many as comparable to the diverse and well-known restaurant industry of its neighbor, New York City. Not only is it on par with the best dining around, it's a relief to have some real food after a week or two of the college cafeteria.

A-

The College Prowler® Grade on

Off-Campus Dining: A-

A high Off-Campus Dining grade implies that off-campus restaurants are affordable, accessible, and worth visiting. Other factors include the variety of cuisine and the availability of alternative options (vegetarian, vegan, Kosher, etc.).

Campus Housing

The Lowdown On... Campus Housing

Undergrads Living on Campus:
72%

Number of Dorms:
18

Number of University-Owned Apartments:
8

Best Dorms:
Alumni Hall
Apartments
Caughlin Hall
Good Counsel Hall
St. Mary's Hall

Worst Dorms:
Fedigan Hall
St. Rita's

→

Dormitories:

Alumni Hall

Floors: 3 plus basement

Total Occupancy: 104

Bathrooms: Shared by floor

Coed: Yes

Residents: Sophomores

Room Types: Single, double, and triple

Special Features: Quiet study hall, Service Learning Community, recreation room, study lounges, laundry, indoor basketball court

Austin Hall

Floors: 3 plus basement

Total Occupancy: 90

Bathrooms: Shared by floor

Coed: Yes

Residents: Juniors and seniors

Room Types: Single

Special Features: Close to dining, library, and classrooms, home to the admission's office, study lounge

Caughlin Hall

Floors: 3

Total Occupancy: 116

Bathrooms: Shared by wing

Coed: No, women only

Residents: Freshmen

Room Types: Double, triple

Special Features: Recreation room, study lounges, laundry, air-conditioning

Corr Hall

Floors: 3

Total Occupancy: 50

Bathrooms: Shared by floor

Coed: Yes

Residents: Sophomores

Room Types: Single

Special Features: Quiet study hall, Career Development Center, counseling center and office for international student advising, bike storage, and laundry

Delurey Hall

Floors: 3 plus basement and sub-ground floor

Total Occupancy: 70

Bathrooms: Shared by floor

Coed: Yes

Residents: Upperclassmen

Room Types: Double, triple

Special Features: Recreation room, study lounge, laundry, basketball courts, politics and Freedom Learning Community

Farley Hall

Floors: 3

Total Occupancy: 156

Bathroom: In room

Coed: Yes

Residents: Juniors and seniors

Room Types: Apartment

Special Features: Air-conditioning, recreation room, study lounge, laundry, fitness center

Fedigan Hall

Floors: 3

Total Occupancy: 120

Bathroom: Shared by floor

Coed: Yes

Residents: Freshmen and sophomores

Room Types: Double

Special Features: Recreation room, study lounge, laundry

Gallen Hall

Floors: 3

Total Occupancy: 156

Bathrooms: In room

Coed: Yes

Residents: Juniors and seniors

Room Types: Apartment

Special Features: Air-conditioning, recreation room, study lounge, laundry

Good Counsel Hall

Floors: 3

Total Occupancy: 240

Bathrooms: Shared by wing

Coed: Yes

Residents: Freshmen and sophomores

Room Types: Double

Special Features: Recreation room, study lounge, laundry, air-conditioning, in-room sinks

Jackson Hall

Floors: 3

Total Occupancy: 156

Bathrooms: In room

(Jackson Hall, continued)

Coed: Yes

Residents: Juniors and seniors

Room Types: Apartment

Special Features: Air-conditioning, recreation room, study lounge, laundry

Klekotka Hall

Floors: 3

Total Occupancy: 156

Bathrooms: In room

Coed: Yes

Residents: Juniors and seniors

Room Types: Apartments

Special Features: Air-conditioning, recreation room, study lounge, laundry

McGuire Hall

Floors: 3

Total Occupancy: 120

Bathrooms: Shared by wing

Coed: No, men only

Residents: Freshmen

Room Types: Double, triple

Special Features: Air-conditioning, recreation room, study lounge, laundry

Moriarty Hall

Floors: 3

Total Occupancy: 50

Bathrooms: Shared by floor

Coed: Yes

Residents: Freshmen

Room Types: Double, triple

(Moriarty Hall, continued)

Special Features: Recreation room, study lounge, laundry

Moulden Hall

Floors: 3

Total Occupancy: 156

Bathrooms: In room

Coed: Yes

Residents: Juniors and seniors

Room Types: Apartment

Special Features: Air-conditioning, recreation room, study lounge, laundry

O'Dwyer Hall

Floors: 3

Total Occupancy: 50

Bathrooms: Shared by floor

Coed: Yes

Residents: Freshmen

Room Types: Double, triple

Special Features: Study lounge, recreation room, laundry

Rudolph Hall

Floors: 3

Total Occupancy: 156

Bathrooms: In room

Coed: Yes

Residents: Juniors and seniors

Room Types: Apartment

Special Features: Air-conditioning, recreation room, study lounge, laundry

St. Clare Hall

Floors: 3

Total Occupancy: 156

Bathrooms: In room

Coed: Yes

Residents: Juniors and seniors

Room Types: Apartment

Special Features: Air-conditioning, recreation room, study lounge, laundry

St. Katharine Hall

Floors: 4

Total Occupancy: 160

Bathrooms: Shared by wing

Coed: No, women only

Residents: Freshmen

Room Types: Double, triple

Special Features: Recreation room, study lounge, laundry

St. Mary's Hall

Floors: 3 plus ground floor and basement

Total Occupancy: 218

Bathrooms: Shared by wing or in room

Coed: Yes

Residents: Upperclassmen

Room Types: Single, double, triple

Special Features: Sinks, chapel, recreation room, study lounge, laundry, cafeteria, pool, gym, home to Second Storey, campus ministry, College of Nursing, and music activities department

St. Monica Hall

Floors: 4

Total Occupancy: 160

Bathrooms: Shared by wing

Coed: No, men only

Residents: Freshmen

Room Types: Double, triple

Special Features: Air-conditioning, recreation room, study lounge, laundry

St. Rita's Hall

Floors: 3 plus basement

Total Occupancy: 50

Bathrooms: Shared by floor

Coed: No, women only

Residents: Juniors and seniors

Room Types: Single

Special Features: Chapel, campus ministry, recreation room, study lounge

Sheehan Hall

Floors: 4

Total Occupancy: 400

Bathrooms: Shared by wing

Coed: Yes

Residents: Sophomores

Room Types: Double, triple

Special Features: Recreation room, study lounge, laundry

Simpson Hall

Floors: 3

Total Occupancy: 30

Bathrooms: Shared by floor

Coed: No, men only

Residents: Freshmen

(Simpson Hall, continued)

Room Types: Double, triple, and quad

Special Features: Recreation room, study lounge, laundry

Stanford Hall

Floors: 5 plus basement

Total Occupancy: 500

Bathrooms: Shared by wing

Coed: Yes

Residents: Freshmen

Room Types: Double

Special Features: Air-conditioning, recreation room, study lounge, laundry, fitness area, campus ministry

Sullivan Hall

Floors: 4

Total Occupancy: 400

Bathrooms: Shared by wing

Coed: Yes

Residents: Sophomores

Room Types: Double, triple, and quad

Special Features: Recreation room, study lounge, laundry

Welsh Hall

Floors: 3

Total Occupancy: 156

Bathrooms: In room

Coed: Yes

Residents: Juniors and seniors

Room Types: Apartment

Special Features: Air-conditioning, recreation room, study lounge, laundry

Room Types:

Single, double, triple, and quad dormitories, as well as apartments that include kitchen, living room, one and a half baths, and two bedrooms for four

Bed Type

Twin extra long (39"x 80"), some lofts, some bunk beds

Available for Rent

Mini-fridge with microwave

Cleaning Service?

In common areas, such as the lounges, hallways, and floor bathrooms. Common areas are cleaned every weekday. On Saturday and Sunday, you are on your own. Apartment bathrooms are not cleaned.

What You Get

A bed, desk and chair, dresser, closet or wardrobe, window coverings, cable TV jack, Ethernet or broadband Internet connections, and free campus calls

Also Available

Smoke-free living option, substance-free housing, learning community housing

Did You Know?

All campus residents get **free cable** and access to Nova's movie channel.

Students Speak Out On... Campus Housing

"Sophomore housing is the best of all four years. You can either live in apartments or off campus your junior year, and by senior year, you must live off campus, but by that point, you are ready."

"The dorms are great. **The best dorms are the junior apartments**. The freshman dorms are also fairly nice. Most of the sophomore dorms are older and not as nice. Overall, they are good. I wouldn't avoid any."

"The freshman dorms range paradoxically—from the really nice, yet extremely strict to the really poor, yet relaxed. While **the older dorms lack air-conditioning and are often cramped**, they have fewer RAs, security guards, and visitation restrictions. The nicer dorms tend to have strict visitation policies."

"**Freshman dorms have a nice selection**. Junior year, the on-campus apartments are amazing. You pay your dues sophomore year. Sophomore year has a limited number of options (mostly just doubles) in small rooms that aren't very impressive. Good dorms have a bad location. Dorms with good locations have a small area."

"Some of the dorms are massive, like Stanford and the Quad dorms. **Some dorms like Simpson and O'Dwyer have less than 75 people in them**. Mostly the bigger dorms are nicer and have more security. The smaller dorms are old and quieter to live in, with less people."

"**I like the size of St. Mary's**. It's an interesting idea to have two rooms. I'll see what it's like next year when I only have one. I love having a sink in my room. I'm right next to the showers, so it's a good location. I recommend all of the dorm's I've seen; they either have good location or good size. They have something for everyone."

"All the freshman dorms are really nice. Stanford probably has the smallest dorms for freshmen, but they are probably bigger then the average-sized dorm. Katharine, **St. Monica, Caughlin, and McGuire all have really nice rooms** complete with air-conditioning."

"**I live in Monica, and I like it** because I was able to make a lot of girl friends. However, the downside to that is that I do not have a lot of guy friends."

"I have to say that **I'm spoiled after living in St. Mary's** since the rooms are very big, and they have their own sinks. Although, I don't think that there are any really bad dorms on campus to live in."

"Dorms vary—**avoid St. Rita's, Fedigan, Moriarty, Simpson, and Austin**. St. Mary's and Good Counsel are the only ones with sinks in the dorms rooms, so they are nice, but people tend to chase after the Quad and the apartments."

"The **dorms are good for the sole reason that the people in them are cool**. No air-conditioning is okay, but they are large and sterile, and at times, impersonal. I like the small ones over the large ones."

"The dorms are not bad. The freshman dorms on Main Campus (O'Dwyer, Delurey, Simpson) do not have air-conditioning. The dorms on South Campus have air-conditioning, and I think the **dorms on West Campus have air-conditioning, as well**."

"All **the dorms have good and bad qualities**. Most freshmen live on South Campus—all air conditioned and roomy dorms. Sophomores mostly live on Main Campus in the Quad, which has smaller rooms, but a great atmosphere, and juniors live in West Campus apartments, which has quad housing with full kitchen and double bathroom options."

The College Prowler Take On... Campus Housing

Since Villanova requires all freshmen to live on campus, making friends is pretty easy. South Campus houses nearly all freshmen, allowing for the majority of freshmen to be familiar with people in their classes. All of the new freshmen dorms have air-conditioning and are comfortable, but they are fairly large, holding no less than 100 people. Another downside is that they are strict about signing in guests. Moriarty and Motown are older buildings in the middle of nowhere. Those who stay there become very close, and there are picnic tables and grills. Security is pretty lax, and no one checks WildCards. On Main Campus, most of the freshmen dorms are off in one corner.

The dorms are comfortable and friendly, giving students a mix between privacy and social environment. Bathrooms are always clean, and there's rarely a wait for showers. Overall, the furniture is in good shape, and the beds are actually pretty comfortable. Whatever shortcomings rooms have, a quick touch-up with some posters and pictures makes rooms more comfortable and inviting. Some smaller dorms become communities all to themselves, and everyone becomes close. In the larger dorms, most have a few close friends and know a whole lot more. It all boils down to preference; if you like less people, look for dorms on Main, and if you like to know a lot of people, South is it. Living on campus is convenient and fun, and few move off before senior year.

B

The College Prowler® Grade on

Campus Housing: B

A high Campus Housing grade indicates that dorms are clean, well-maintained, and spacious. Other determining factors include variety of dorms, proximity to classes, and social atmosphere.

Off-Campus Housing

The Lowdown On... Off-Campus Housing

Undergrads in Off-Campus Housing:
28%

Average Rent For:
1BR Apt.: $675/month
2BR Apt.: $930/month
3BR Apt.: $1200/month

Best Time to Look for a Place:
End of first semester

Popular Areas:
Ardmore
Bryn Mawr

For Assistance, Contact:
Office of Residence Life
(610) 519-4154
www.villanova.edu/studentlife/reslife/offcampus
residencelife@villanova.edu

Students Speak Out On...
Off-Campus Housing

"Living on campus is the best idea for the first three years of school. The dorms are great, and they're obviously the most convenient pick."

"There is no guaranteed four-year housing on campus, unless you are: a presidential scholar, a varsity athlete, a nursing student, or a female engineer. The transition to moving off campus senior year is greatly facilitated by Residence Life, who provide the students with plenty of options and suggestions. **Moving off campus really teaches you how to deal with things** like rent and leases. It's a good learning experience."

"**Finding off-campus housing is a bit of a hassle**, plus you isolate yourself from student life. I wouldn't recommend living off campus until you have to."

"**Villanova guarantees housing for three years**. However, some, myself included, hope to escape the bridles of dorm life. As a freshman currently looking to move off campus, I can tell you it's not easy to find a place that is both affordable and desirable. By the time most students decide whether they want to move off campus or not, they are months behind in the search."

"Off-campus housing doesn't really become a major issue until junior year. But by **the time junior year comes, everyone wants to live in the on-campus apartments**. Senior year is the main year for living off campus."

"I've heard that it's **not even cheaper to go off campus**. Then you have the problem of landlords who are a bigger pain then your RA. You also don't get as much of the college experience. I would not recommend living off campus until senior year. I think by then you will need to learn how to deal with landlords."

"**Sophomore year everyone lives on Main Campus, and it is quite convenient**. I have one friend who is living off campus next year with a few junior friends, but pretty much everyone lives on campus. It's not worth the hassle, given the fact that most sophomores live on campus. Some juniors live off if they don't get to live in the apartments, and all seniors live off campus."

"Villanova does not guarantee senior housing. So many people do live off campus that it is convenient to find an apartment and a roommate. **It is worth living off campus your senior year**, and most juniors enjoy the apartments on West Campus."

The College Prowler Take On...
Off-Campus Housing

There are a lot of places to choose from in the nearby area, but the only problem is finding one in time. With the freedom of off-campus living comes bills and commuting. While Villanova is home to two rail lines and three train stations, getting to school can be a pain. It isn't in walking distance, and transportation can get expensive. Most are scattered over many towns, including Wayne, Bryn Mawr, Rosemont, and Ardmore. A popular place is the Courts in nearby Bryn Mawr, but the wait to get in is backed up several years. Hanging out with friends can be as much of a pain as commuting to school. Problems aside, living off campus provides loads of freedom and proves to be a fun and memorable experience.

It's not too hard to find a place, and Residence Life helps ease the transition to living on your own. At the beginning of each semester, they post housing opportunities and a checklist of things to look for when inspecting housing. Houses that are entirely rented out to college students sometimes have backyards, which offer you more freedom and room to move around. Make sure they fit what you are looking for, and make sure it's suitable for living and the prices are fair. Get a feel for the neighborhood, because some residents are not big fans of college students and will be quick to call the cops at any sign of a party, and the cops are even less friendly to college students.

A-

The College Prowler® Grade on

Off-Campus Housing: A-

A high grade in Off-Campus Housing indicates that apartments are of high quality, close to campus, affordable, and easy to secure.

Diversity

The Lowdown On... Diversity

African American:
5%

Asian American:
6%

Hispanic:
6%

International:
2%

Native American:
Less than 1%

White:
77%

Unknown:
3%

Out-of-State:
71%

Political Activity

It is difficult to say where most students fall. Many, due to background, tend to lean more conservatively, but there is also a sizable amount of liberals on campus. In terms of clubs, Villanova has a chapter of the College Republicans and College Democrats, as well as the Democratic Socialists of America, but all three are fairly low-key.

Gay Pride

Acceptance of homosexuality is a fairly touchy subject at Villanova. While most students are accepting of gay classmates, the University is Catholic, and as such, follows the teachings of the Catholic Church. That is not to say, however, that there are no forums for gay and straight students interested in gay issues. Villanova's campus ministry sponsors BGLOV (Bisexual and Gay students of Villanova), as well as a gay/straight coalition.

Most Popular Religions

The most popular religion by far is Roman Catholicism. Augustinians founded the school, and their sentiments are echoed through institutions like Campus Ministry and the Office for Mission Effectiveness. However, Campus Ministry also provides transportation for any students who wish to attend services of another faith.

Economic Status

Villanova, like most other schools, has students from a few diverse backgrounds. However, students sometimes attack the school as being full of rich white kids.

Minority Clubs

Villanova's minority clubs always put on great events that range from being highly educational to entertaining. Clubs like SAMOSA and VISA are a few examples of organizations on campus that play an important role in promoting the small minority populations around the University.

Students Speak Out On...
Diversity

"The moniker Vanilla-nova is deserved. Almost everyone is white, almost everyone is Catholic. It's one of the qualities I dislike most about Villanova."

"The **campus is almost all white people**, hence the name Vanilla-nova."

"At first glance, Villanova might not seem very diverse, but if you look in the right way, you can find it. Villanova has a wide range of students from all over the country. Although it's a joke that everyone is from New Jersey, that's far from true. There is a large west coast contingency, as well as an impressive number of Hispanic students. **Although people might not look and see an obvious diversity, it is present**."

"It's a little more diverse then my high school, but some **people complain and call it Vanilla-nova**. I don't really think that's true."

"The campus is **not very diverse** at all."

"Basically, they **don't call it Vanilla-nova for nothing**."

"**Villanova is not as diverse** in appearance as in thought, perhaps."

"Villanova gets a lot of flak for not being very diverse, but generally, that is a statement by people who do not know any better. **There are students on campus from at least 48 states and 14 countries**. While it may seem like one group of people dominate the campus, this could not be farther from the truth. We cater greatly to diversity, both ethnically and culturally. There are plenty of associations and clubs dealing with diversity on campus, and the University does a lot to change its bad reputation for being homogenous."

"Villanova's problem is the **lack of diversity** on campus. The majority of people I met here are just from the tri-state area, and everyone gets along."

"Vanilla-nova! There is **slim to no diversity**, and until there are people from different economic backgrounds, we will not be able to become more diverse."

"The campus is barely diverse, but I have seen Villanova take so many strides to make it more diverse. **Villanova always sponsors diversity lectures**, overnight trips to those of other backgrounds looking at the school, and a mandatory presentation dedicated to this issue held during orientation. I definitely have to commend Villanova on its efforts taken towards this issue."

"**Villanova + diversity = no**. They don't call it Vanilla-nova for nothing."

The College Prowler Take On... Diversity

Villanova's reputation concerning diversity is something that can definitely be criticized. While there are international students and minorities here, overall these comprise a very small percent of the schools population. Generally, the international student population is synonymous with the minority students. The majority of students who attend are white, with very similar economic, educational, ethnic, geographic, and religious backgrounds. A large group of students are Catholic and tend to be from Irish or Italian decent. Villanova leans heavily on the tri-state for students, and the students from the areas of the nation can probably be counted in a thousand or less. However, the minority organizations, as well as the administration, have been working hard on increasing awareness and diversity around campus, and every year, they try to make Villanova that much more diverse.

The only positive aspect of diversity at the University is the male to female ratio. The numbers are almost even. If you want diversity, it's best to leave campus and head to Philadelphia to experience the wide array of cultures present there. Overall, the nearby area's diversity makes up for the seemingly "vanilla" makeup of the school.

D+

The College Prowler® Grade on

Diversity: D+

A high grade in Diversity indicates that ethnic minorities and international students have a notable presence on campus and that students of different economic backgrounds, religious beliefs, and sexual preferences are well-represented.

Guys & Girls

The Lowdown On...
Guys & Girls

Male Undergrads:
49%

Female Undergrads:
51%

Birth Control Available?

No, following Roman Catholic doctrine, as well as the spirit of the Augustinian mission, no form of birth control is offered on campus or through any organization with school affiliation.

Social Scene

There is always something to do on campus, and Villanova has a diverse and prevalent social scene. Almost all of the students are friendly and open to meeting new people. By this token, it is very easy to just walk around a dorm and make friends with almost everyone there. Also, the University facilitates the social atmosphere further with CAT, the Campus Activities Team, which has something planned for every weekend that the school is in session. Examples are concerts with headliner bands, battle of local bands, Novafest, and open-mic night.

Hookups or Relationships?

It's about even between hookups and relationships. First-year students coming in probably have a more sizable population of those in long-distance relationships, but that usually changes by second semester. In any event, whether you are on the prowl for some long-term commitments or just looking for a hookup on a weekend, both are equally represented around campus, enough that neither group is unhappy.

Best Place to Meet Guys/Girls

With such a large population of students who volunteer their time, it is not surprising that meeting people through extracurricular activities plays such a large role in relationships on campus. Often, students also meet people through study groups, classes, or close friends. Since the student body is fairly small, it's not unusual to meet someone through a friend or a friend of a friend. But if sitting around and waiting is not your thing, there are always the parties on the weekend to meet people. Since dorm parties are the most common on campus, hookups are usually with people you know or have a mutual friend with. Another good place to find hotties is on Sheehan Beach. The only problem is they don't come out until late spring when it's warm enough to wear those more revealing clothes in attempts to catch a tan or air out in the warm weather. But the hotties are never in short supply, and anyone with a little determination will have no problem in spotting plenty—regardless of season, temperature, or extracurricular activities you've joined.

Dress Code

More often than not, a comment is that Villanova looks like a modeling agency for Abercrombie & Fitch. While there is a fair amount of diversity when it comes to dress, and there is hardly a dress code, most students rock their Abercrombie shirts with a pair of jeans or khakis. Another popular clothing brand is Hollister. That is not to say that you won't see the sweatshirt or sweatpants being worn during the winter or spring. Even with a mix, most students tend to dress preppy.

Did You Know?

Top Places to Find Hotties:

1. Parties
2. Class
3. Sheehan Beach and Stanford Hill
5. The Quad

Top Places to Hook Up:

1. The makeout tree
2. Dorm parties
3. Empty classrooms
4. Organization parties off campus

Students Speak Out On...
Guys & Girls

"Typical prepsters! If you are into that, you will love it—many hot preppy sorority girls, all beautiful—but if you search, you can find alternative beauty."

"Going to **Villanova University will make the girls you hook up with back home seem ugly**. As a guy, your standards rise at Villanova, which leads to the common misperception that the girls are prudes; they aren't, you are just going after girls a lot better looking than you. In the long run, it works out, though; you spit better game back home, and you hook up with hotter girls here."

"It's like anywhere else. There are good-looking people, and there are not. It has been said that Villanova students dress for class like they would for a fashion show, but you do see people in more relaxed clothes, as well. **You can find any type of person at Villanova**; there's a definite variety, even if you don't think so at first."

"The majority of guys and girls at Villanova are friendly and intelligent. Of course, there are some people to avoid, but that is just a fact of life. Heck yeah, **the girls are hot at Villanova**!"

"I have found that **the girls here can be cliquey, materialistic, and very predictable**. The guys who are on varsity sports teams seem to only hang out with teammates."

"Preppy guys and flirty girls from the middle- to upper-class America—**of course we're hot**."

"**Guys are hot, and the girls are hot, too**. Basically Villanova is an Abercrombie catalog, and if that does it for you, go for it."

"**Everyone at Villanova is very preppy**, and I am guessing this comes from private school backgrounds, dressing up everyday. The time put into making yourself up is definitely evident, though."

"I guess the guys and girls are good. And yes, **the girls are hot**."

"On average, **the guys here are remarkably short**. The reason is unknown for this lack in height. Granted, there are tall basketball and football players that tower over you in the food line, but all the non-athletes are noticeably shorter than the average college-aged male."

"Oh yeah, **this is a great-looking campus**. Everyone is really nice looking here."

The College Prowler Take On...
Guys & Girls

Walk around for five minutes, and there will be no doubt that the overwhelming majority of students on campus are hot. With an almost perfect balance of male and female students, there is always someone out there you haven't met. While students are in session for the colder months, that doesn't stop most of the people from looking good. All around, the campus is well dressed year round, and this can be both a good and bad thing. In either case, both sexes are just an added benefit of going to the school.

Most guys and girls are intelligent, caring people who are nice and fun to be around. Whether you're coming to Villanova in search of a special someone or just a hookup on the weekend, there is a roughly even balance between both. While there are other schools in the area that offer new faces outside Villanova, it's often difficult for underclassmen to go to events or places that offer this. Based on that and the fact that the University is the largest in the area, most relationships past freshman year are restricted to the campus. However, some take their chances at UPenn for a weekend of fun and just something to do outside Villanova's campus.

A-

The College Prowler® Grade on

Guys: A-

A high grade for Guys indicates that the male population on campus is attractive, smart, friendly, and engaging, and that the school has a decent ratio of guys to girls.

A

The College Prowler® Grade on

Girls: A

A high grade for Girls not only implies that the women on campus are attractive, smart, friendly, and engaging, but also that there is a fair ratio of girls to guys.

Athletics

The Lowdown On... Athletics

Athletic Division:
NCAA Division I

Conference:
Big East

School Mascot:
Wildcat

Men Playing Varsity Sports:
305 (10%)

Women Playing Varsity Sports:
309 (9%)

Men's Varsity Sports:

Baseball
Basketball
Cross country
Football
Golf
Lacrosse
Soccer
Swimming and diving
Tennis
Track and field

Women's Varsity Sports:

Basketball
Cross country
Field hockey
Lacrosse
Rowing
Soccer
Softball
Swimming and diving
Tennis
Track and field
Volleyball
Water polo

Club Sports:

Basketball (women's)
Cheerleading
Crew
Cycling
Equestrian
Field hockey
Golf

(Club Sports, continued)

Ice hockey
Judo
Karate
Lacrosse
Sailing
Skiing and snowboarding
Soccer
Surfing
Tennis
Ultimate Frisbee
Volleyball (men's)
Water Polo (men's)

Intramurals:

5K race
Aerobics
Basketball
Billards
Dodgeball
Flag football
Soccer (indoor and outdoor)
Softball
Ultimate Frisbee
Volleyball (court and sand)
Whiffleball

Extramurals:

City 6 5K race
City 6 basketball
City 6 flag football
City 6 softball
City 6 volleyball

Athletic Fields

Mendel Field, Villanova Sports Complex, Villanova Stadium

Getting Tickets

For football, each student just needs to show his or her WildCard to get in. For basketball, every student needs to enter a lottery roughly a week before each game. Instructions on how to enter the lottery and results are always done through e-mail. For every other sport, seating is generally not an issue.

Most Popular Sports

Villanova lives and dies by basketball. Purchasing tickets for games in the Pavilion have up to a five-year wait. Men's has a larger following, but women's also gets a decent amount of fans per game. Games are intense, and they are usually fun whether the team comes out with a win or loss. Football is also fairly popular, with the Parent's Weekend and Alumni Weekend being the most crowded games.

Overlooked Teams

Men's baseball, women's softball, men's and women's track

Best Place to Take a Walk

Villanova Stadium, around campus

Gyms/Facilities

West Gym

West Gym is in the basement of Farley Hall and houses aerobic machines and free and universal weights. However, most of the aerobic equipment is, more often than not, broken, and those that do work have ridiculous waits. During peak hours, the gym gets crowded, so you have to wait to lift.

South Gym

Housed in the basement of Stanford on South Campus, the gym has the same difficulties as West Gym. However, the more dedicated lifters should go here, as there is a wider selection of free weights, and the equipment allows for more weight on all of the universal machines. But the aerobic equipment, as with West, tends to be broken or has extremely long waits.

Jake Nevin Field House

The field house does not hold any gyms, but it does have several indoor basketball and volleyball courts, as well as a pool in the basement. It is an older building, though, and it is often difficult to find any of the facilities the first time around.

Outdoor Tennis, Volleyball, and Basketball Courts

Every dorm on campus is within a two-minute walk of a tennis, volleyball, or basketball court, and there is an area that has a combination of each. On West Campus, students can go to St. Mary's where there are indoor basketball/volleyball courts, as well as a pool. Also on West are outdoor sandpits for volleyball and basketball courts that are lit for a pickup game anytime of the night. On Main, there are scores of basketball/tennis courts, the largest outdoor grouping being found behind the Quad.

Students Speak Out On... Athletics

"Sports are great fun for everyone here. Season football tickets are given out to all students, and while they don't generally produce a good turnout, the games are a lot of fun."

"Basketball tickets are distributed on a lottery system based on your attendance at previous games, and they are usually not that difficult to get if you're a loyal fan. **Intramural and club sports are very big on campus**, there is just about every sport offered intramurally. The club teams are just a step below varsity and are very competitive without the time commitment."

"**Villanova lives and dies with the basketball team**. Intramurals are awesome. I participate in IM soccer, play Capoeria with the Villanova Capoeria club, and play club rugby."

"Basketball is the thing to do around here, but football is catching up. **IM sports seem to do fairly well**, too."

"**Sports are a huge part of campus life**, especially basketball and football."

"I think **football and basketball are the most interesting** sports. I've gone to a few games of each, but not to anything else."

"Sports are big, but not too big. **You have a following for basketball and football**, enough to where it is a good time to go to the games."

"Basketball is the thing! It's funny, because the football team is very good, but they don't get the same recognition. **Basketball games are tons of fun**. The student section is ridiculous—always rowdy. I recommend attending at least one basketball game (men's and women's teams) during your Villanova career."

"Everyone goes to football games and men's basketball games. I would like to see more people get interested in women's basketball because they are really good. I am on the women's club lacrosse team, and I really like it. It's **hard to get turf time because of the varsity sports**, but overall, it's going pretty well."

"**Football and basketball games are widely attended**. Intramural sports are fun if you get a good group of friends to play."

"The basketball games are fun to go to, because our basketball team is semi-competitive. The **football games aren't that great**. Intramural sports are pretty popular—most dorms send a few teams for each sport."

"The big varsity sports such as football, and especially basketball, attract a ton of people to games. For basketball, they lottery out tickets so that everyone gets a fair chance to attend the games. Intramural sports are pretty big, as well. I have played on intramural basketball and softball, and **it's a good way to get out and just have some fun**."

"**Basketball is very popular**, and the games are tons of fun."

The College Prowler Take On... Athletics

One thing to be said about Villanova athletics is that the campus eats, sleeps, and breathes by the men's basketball team. Steeped in tradition, basketball games are a guaranteed fun time, even if you don't like sports in the slightest. Basketball is so celebrated that if the team wins a big game against one of the schools rivals, especially St. Joseph's, they come back as heroes for a day. Followed up in a distant second is the football program. Due to the fact that the football program is Division I-AA, it attracts lesser-known teams, but at the cost of playing a Division I-A game. The games to watch in football would be the University of Delaware game, as well as whoever they play on Parent's Weekend and Alumni Weekend.

But varsity athletics is only one of the many outlets for students who want to stay in shape and have lots of fun doing it. Intramurals are big for those who are involved. While most games don't carry the intensity of a Final Four game, they are fun to watch and even more fun to play in. They are, overall, a great way to stay in shape while hanging out with your friends and meeting new people. The athletics here at Villanova are source of both entertainment and fun year round.

A-

The College Prowler® Grade on

Athletics: A-

A high grade in Athletics indicates that students have school spirit, that sports programs are respected, that games are well-attended, and that intramurals are a prominent part of student life.

Nightlife

The Lowdown On...
Nightlife

Club and Bar Prowler: Popular Nightlife Spots!

Club Crawler:

The nightclubs in Philadelphia are fun, but most close at 2 a.m. The following are the best nightclubs in the city and are packed with college students, native Philadelphians, young professionals, and the occasional old person trying to relive their youth.

Chrome

939 N. Delaware Ave.
Philadelphia

(215) 931-0101

Student organizations are always pulling together a few buses and heading over to Chrome on weekend nights. There are huge dance floors, with hip-hop, rap, and house. 17 to enter, 21 to drink, with live DJs, definitely a must-to during your first few months in the Philly area.

➜

Club Flow

700 N. Columbus Blvd.
Philadelphia

(215) 923-0504

www.clubflowonline.com

Club Flow is great, and it is easy on the college student's pocket. Hosting great parties throughout the week, Club Flow offers up an interesting array of music and people, attracting a large, diverse, cultural crowd. Thursdays are by far the best night to hit up Club Flow, with cheap drinks and tons of college students.

Ice Nite Club

1160 First Ave.
King of Prussia

(610) 878-8483

www.iceniteclub.com

A quality club outside Philadelphia, it's a great place for Mainline students who don't want to travel into Philly for the night. With a wide range of music, good drink specials, and great theme parties like "Fresh Squeezed Fridays," and "Go Saturdays," it's a fun time and always packed with college students and Mainline locals. The best day to hit up Ice is definitely on Fridays.

Bar Crawler:

Bars of all types are really popular for the Mainline and Philly. For 'Nova students, drink specials are a must. Most Villanovans go to the following bars:

Brownies

23 E. Lancaster Ave.
Ardmore

(610) 649-8389

www.brownies23east.com

Not too far from campus, with drink specials almost every day of the week and live music as a backdrop, it's never hard to find a Villanovan or two around the bar. Drink specials range from 50 cent drafts to $2 bottles.

Callahan's Irish Pub

7681 Frankford Ave.
Philadelphia

(215) 338-4188

www.callahansirishpub.com

Its atmosphere is rich in Irish culture and heritage. With daily drink specials and live DJs on the weekend, you can't go wrong coming here. There is also live traditional Irish music, karaoke nights, and game nights.

Erin's Pub

36 W. Winona Ave.
Norwood

(610) 461-0991

On the way to Philly, Erin's is a great place to sit down, relax, and meet up with friends. Drink specials are decent, with the best specials on Thursdays and Fridays. Very popular among Villanova students.

Grog Restaurant & Bar

863 W. Lancaster Ave.
Bryn Mawr

(610) 527-5870

An upscale bar and restaurant right on the Mainline, it is very popular for Villanova students, as well as other local schools. An old building with great ambience and a good assortment of delicious food, it has a full bar filled with domestic and imported drinks and beers. Located near a lot of off-campus housing and just a short drive from campus, there are 'Nova students in there almost every day of the week.

The Wild Onion

900 Conestoga Rd.
Bryn Mawr

(610) 527-4826

The Wild Onion offers a laid-back atmosphere catering to college students. Nestled close to campus and off-campus housing, it's never hard to spot a few people you know somewhere in the bar. Complementing the bar is a decent selection of food with killer wings. Also, the Wild Onion has DJs to liven things up.

Useful Resources for Nightlife

www.phillyatnight.com

www.philadelphia.com/nightlife

Philadelphia Inquirer

Philadelphia Magazine

Other Places to Check Out:

Attic
The Barn
Continental Restaurant & Martini Bar
Déjà Vu
Dirty Frank's
Dock Street Brewing
Electric Factory
Fergie's Pub
Irish Pub
J.C. Dobbs
Jake and Oliver's
John Harvard's Brew House
Katmandu
McGullicuddy's
The Warehouse
Xero

Student Favorites:

Grog Restaurant & Bar
The Wild Onion

Cheapest Place to Get a Drink:

Grog Restaurant & Bar

Primary Areas with Nightlife:

Delaware and South Street
The Mainline

Bars Close At:

2 a.m.

Favorite Drinking Games:

Beer Pong
Card Games (Kings)
Power Hour
Quarters

House Parties

House parties are not all that common unless you are a junior or senior and live off campus. The police in the area tend to come down hard on off-campus parties, so people often avoid throwing them. Those parties that do happen, though, tend to be restricted to people from a club or organization, not to mention quite a distance from campus. The more favored form of partying is getting a few friends to come over to your dorm room on the weekend for a small, but fun, gathering.

Organization Parties

Organization sponsored parties are a great way to enjoy yourself and meet new people. Ranging from cocktails (popular among the sororities) to renting out clubs by the fraternities, almost every organization hosts some type of party throughout the year. As an underclassman, this is probably the best bet for getting into the nightlife at Villanova.

What to Do if You're Not 21

Theater of the Living Arts (TLA)

344 South St., Philadelphia
(215) 922-1011
www.theateroflivingarts.net

While not a club, the TLA provides a great outlet for dancing and just a straight-up enjoyable time. TLA hosts a variety of venues ranging from large headliner bands to lesser-known local artists. Venues range from pop rock to indie rock, underground hip-hop to rap. TLA usually hosts events at least five times a week, cost varying on the artist. Located right on the ever-famous South Street, there is always plenty to do before and after a show, with numerous places to eat and shop.

The Trocadero

1003 Arch St., Philadelphia
(215) 922-LIVE
www.thetroc.com

Much like TLA, the Trocadero holds a variety of musical venues ranging from underground rock and hip-hop to major headliners like D-12, Badly Drawn Boy, and the John Butler Trio. However, every Monday, they play movies for an affordable price, drinks and food included. The Troc is also a little more affordable than TLA, having few, if any, shows that break $20 a ticket.

Students Speak Out On...
Nightlife

"There are always plenty of parties on campus, and they tend to stay rather small due to the great RAs doing their duty of breaking up too much noise."

"Off-campus parties also occur in the surrounding towns, mostly held by seniors that live off campus in apartment complexes. **There are a ton of bars** on the Mainline, and every night of the week has different drink specials, so the students typically just rotate around those establishments depending on the night."

"You can always find a party on campus at Villanova. As far as the clubs go, **Villanova often offers discounts to certain clubs** in Philadelphia, which include buses to and from the club."

"**Parties on campus are decent**. There are usually several parties during the weekends in the junior apartments. Off-campus bars are very popular among upperclassmen. These bars include Erin's, Brownies, the Grog, and the Onion."

"Unless you are in the dorm, which is hard to manage, there are **not a ton of good places to party on campus**. There are no frat houses on campus, although most of the frats rent out a place in Philly and sell tickets to these parties. The Barn is a big place. If not heading out to the frat scene, then bars are definitely another option. There are a ton of bars on the Mainline, including McGullicuddy's and Erin's Pub."

"The **parties on campus are horrible**. There are no frat houses on campus, so you need to go off campus to go to a party, and that can get expensive and annoying, but the bars are fun."

"The parties on and off campus are loads of fun. There are a **great variety of clubs of bars to go to in Philly**. I do not know any names of good spots, since I don't drink and don't go to bars, but there are many activities for non-drinkers like the movies, King of Prussia Mall, and plays."

"There are no parties on campus. You will be written up if you have a party. All of the **parties are off campus and require you to buy an expensive ticket**, and take a sketchy bus ride to an unknown place. The party scene is completely different from all other colleges. If you want frat parties on campus where you pay $5 or nothing to get in, don't come here. Most of the juniors and seniors have fun at the bars up Lancaster Avenue in Bryn Mawr."

"Parties on campus are good. There's never a huge one, just because space doesn't really allow it. **Frats do rent out clubs where they run buses and have open bars** and stuff. The area is great for the bar scene, but the better bars are really tough about 21 and over."

"**Villanova is not a party school** at all! You must always pay, and must always go off campus. Most of the time, a frat will rent out a club for the night at $25 a pop, which gets expensive."

"The parties are alright, but most of the people just drink in their rooms, though. I like **Beta parties, those tend to be fun**. I think the frat houses are small and maybe should expand a bit."

"**I do not like doing most of the school sponsored club events, because they are a rip off**. Plus, all of the bars are relatively strict."

"If you are a party guy or gal at Villanova, you either need a fake ID or need to get involved with an organization. Dorm room parties get old quick. Join a fraternity or sorority, not because they have great, really huge parties, but because they are a great connection to a lot of fun gatherings. **The group with the best rep for partying is undoubtedly the rugby team**."

"**Parties off campus are hit or miss**. I would not know about bars, because of the carding and the checking of IDs here is ridiculous. There are some cool places in the city, though."

The College Prowler Take On...
Nightlife

Sometimes accused of being Villa-no-fun, it is often difficult for underclassmen to tap into the rich nightlife surrounding Philadelphia. As you get older, your opportunities increase dramatically. With a limited selection of under-21 locations, it's always a safe bet to see what's going on at the local venues like the Troc. Both are a great way of meeting people and having fun—and all at an affordable rate. While there is no unofficial Villanova bar, students tend to frequent those located directly on the Mainline.

And until that 21 birthday, nightlife is pretty limited. However, Villanova does an admirable job of providing entertainment on campus. Check out Connelly Center, because there is almost always some type of free event. Dorm room parties tend to be small and can get boring. As an underclassman, your best bet is to join an organization. They sponsor events and rent out venues and provide ways to meet new people. By sophomore year, students generally know enough upperclassmen to end up at a party. Junior and senior years are by far the best years for nightlife, as there are little restrictions on venues, with free reign to the clubs and bars in Philadelphia.

B

The College Prowler® Grade on

Nightlife: B

A high grade in Nightlife indicates that there are many bars and clubs in the area that are easily accessible and affordable. Other determining factors include the number of options for the under-21 crowd and the prevalence of house parties.

Greek Life

The Lowdown On...
Greek Life

Number of Fraternities:
10

Undergrad Men in Fraternities:
12%

Number of Sororities:
9

Undergrad Women in Sororities:
33%

Fraternities:

Beta Theta Phi
Delta Tau Delta
Phi Gamma Delta
Phi Sigma Kappa
Sigma Alpha Epsilon
Sigma Alpha Mu
Sigma Chi
Sigma Nu
Sigma Pi
Zeta Psi

Sororities:

Alpha Chi Omega
Alpha Delta Pi
Alpha Phi
Chi Omega
Delta Delta Delta
Delta Gamma
Kappa Delta
Kappa Kappa Gamma
Pi Beta Phi

Multicultural Colonies:

Alpha Kappa Alpha
Alpha Phi Alpha
Kappa Alpha Psi

Other Greek Organizations:

Greek Council
Interfraternity Council
Order of Omega
Pan-Hellenic Council

Students Speak Out On... Greek Life

"Greek life here is much weaker than most other college campuses, because there are no Greek houses. So, it does not dominate the social scene, but it does give you a chance to make more friends."

"**Greek life is a large part of Villanova**, however, it definitely doesn't dominate the social scene. There are plenty of other events and organizations to get involved with that aren't associated with Greek life."

"Since there are no Greek houses, it doesn't really dominate the scene, but it can if you want it to. I think **Nova has a nice balance** between Greek and non-Greek."

"Greek life on campus is in a sorry state. The University is **extremely strict on the on-campus fraternities**. More students prefer 'off-campus,' or 'underground' frats, which don't heed to the University. Connection to frats and sororities are important to freshmen in order to find off-campus parties, but later on, they lose importance."

"I **don't think Greek life dominates**. There are a lot of people that aren't in Greek life, and even if they are, they still hang out with non-Greek life people. It's not like a cult or anything."

"The alternatives make fun of Greek life. The Greekers love it and every aspect of the life they have gotten themselves into. You don't need it. Basically, **you pay $200 a month to have guaranteed friends**. I say get some self-confidence, and you'll be fine."

"The Greek life is present, but not suffocating. **It's much larger for women than men**. Because there are no on-campus houses, Greek life is almost like just another club you can be a part of. It's a great program if you'd like to take part in Greek life, but it's not something you feel you have to be a part of."

"Greek life does not dominate the social scene, but it is available. I felt that I needed to join a sorority in order to find a group of girls that I felt comfortable with. Also, the social scene that I was experiencing prior to the sorority was not what I envisioned. **Drinking in someone's room seemed pretty lame compared to frat parties**."

"Greek organizations take over the Spit two or three nights a week and are very loud. The **sororities are very cliquey and categorize the girls** who are in them."

"There is absolutely **no Greek housing on campus**, which provides an atmosphere where sororities and fraternities do not dominate. The people who are in these groups are involved in many other activities and really mix in with the rest of the Villanova community. They are great groups to get involved with, as they all support philanthropies, as well as hold countless social events to get to know other students, but they are not exclusive."

"**Greek life can seem like a big part of Villanova**, but it is really what you make it out to be. The frats are really open to anyone coming to the functions, and the sororities definitely do not separate themselves from the rest of campus."

"Greek life is popular, but it definitely does not dominate the social scene. **There is a lot you can do and experience without joining a fraternity or sorority**."

The College Prowler Take On... Greek Life

Students looking for an *Animal House* or *Old School* fraternity are looking in the wrong place. Villanova Greek life is treated like any other club or organization throughout campus. Greek rivalries are nonexistent on campus. Most Greeks have friends in and outside their fraternities and sororities. Greek life offers a great way to meet new people and form close relationships. Another big thing that Villanova's Greek life is into is philanthropy work. Most spend a couple weekends helping out the underprivileged or raising money for charities, as well as fun events.

However, if it's the party scene you are interested in, Villanova's Greek life makes only a small dent. Due to no on-campus Greek housing, most only throw parties on occasion. For popular events, they rent out a club or bar and charge a small cover. Sororities tend to revolve around formals or cocktail-type events. Many parties off campus are usually broken up by the police within an hour or two, not to mention that none are in walking distance. While Greek life at Villanova offers a great way to meet new people, it is hardly treated any differently than most clubs and organizations, even by the Greeks themselves.

B

The College Prowler® Grade on

Greek Life: B

A high grade in Greek Life indicates that sororities and fraternities are not only present, but also active on campus. Other determining factors include the variety of houses available and the respect the Greek community receives from the rest of the campus.

Drug Scene

The Lowdown On... Drug Scene

Most Prevalent Drugs on Campus:
Alcohol
Cocaine
Marijuana

Alcohol-Related Referrals:
830

Alcohol-Related Arrests:
7

Drug-Related Referrals:
36

Drug-Related Arrests:
6

Drug Counseling Programs

Alcoholic Anonymous

(610) 519-7407

Meets weekly to discuss dependency on alcohol

The Center for Health and Wellness Education

(610) 519-7407

Provides evaluations to assess dependency, referral to counseling, library containing informational packets, books, and videos concerning alcohol and drug related issues

Office of Alcohol & Drug Assistance

(610) 519-7407

Alcohol assessment services, individual and group counseling, educational materials

Peers Offering Wellness & Educational Resources (POWER)

(610) 519-7407

Peer involvement in education, and counseling in drugs and alcohol, sexual health, and harrassment

The University Counseling Center

(610) 519-4050

Confidential counseling for students wishing to address alcohol or drug related concerns

Students Speak Out On...
Drug Scene

"The most common drugs are coke and pot. There is not a whole lot more. Alcohol is huge, but where is it not?"

"**I haven't seen people do anything more than weed**, but it's easy to stay away from and easy to get involved in. It's totally up to the person; they should be able to make wise or unwise decisions."

"No matter where you go live, there is a drug scene. However, at Villanova it is **very tough to find, unless it is sought out**. It is definitely not something that is prominent, and you can go through your entire time here and never see it."

"Personally, **I have not found there to be a ton of drugs at Villanova at all**. I have seen a little pot here and there. But other than that, to my surprise, I haven't seen anything other than that at all."

"The **drug scene is just like any other college** campus. There is drinking and use of other drugs, as well."

"Every campus has a drug problem. Villanova's drug problem is not too bad, because **security is really tight** if you are doing drugs or drinking. Villanova is a dry campus, so watch out for Public Safety. Never do drugs period, because you will be caught, and may be kicked out of school."

"I know that the drugs exist, but I have not experienced them firsthand. **I think that those who smoke weed are pretty quiet about it**."

"**Pot is probably the largest drug on campus**. It's cheap and easy to get. However, Villanova is a wealthy school with lots of rich kids, so harder drugs can be found. If you're looking for drugs, you'd probably be able to find them, if you're not, then you'll probably only notice some marijuana."

"Alcohol consumption is comparable with that of other schools. Occasionally, marijuana is encountered, as well. Overall, **there is not as much drug use as other schools**, especially where narcotics are concerned."

"There are a few people who do drugs, but **I don't think it's a serious problem or anything**."

"I have never had trouble getting drunk on campus when I wanted. You just need to be persistent and know kids. As for drugs, **softer drugs are commonplace**, but by no means dominate. I've heard rumors of cocaine usage."

The College Prowler Take On...
Drug Scene

Drug use on campus is hardly a visible presence, and most of those that do it aren't doing it daily. However, you can occasionally run into the softer drugs somewhere on campus, but again, this is not a daily occurrence. Of course, there are the few kids who just sit around and smoke up all day, but it will require a search to find these kids. The drug of choice on campus by far is alcohol, as it is the most common and most accessible. The use of any type of drugs can become problematic if you are not intelligent about your use of them, because the police are pretty strict since Villanova is a dry campus.

Villanova has about the same amount of drug use as your average college or high school, and there is no pressure to get involved. While there are rumors that there is a heavy cocaine-using population on campus, there are few occasions where people are seen using it. Getting your hands on drugs isn't overly complicated. If you are looking for drugs, they are not hard to find, but it is not something prevalent on campus. If you don't do it, no one is going to bother you.

B+

The College Prowler® Grade on

Drug Scene: B+

A high grade in the Drug Scene indicates that drugs are not a noticeable part of campus life; drug use is not visible, and no pressure to use them seems to exist.

Campus Strictness

The Lowdown On...
Campus Strictness

What Are You Most Likely to Get Caught Doing on Campus?

- Drinking underage
- Hall sports
- Having candles and incense sticks in your dorm room
- Making too much noise in your dorm
- Parking illegally
- Possession of alcohol
- Public urination or indecency

Students Speak Out On... Campus Strictness

"Campus is so strict! You will be screwed if you are not careful. Be smart. Radnor police are out to get you, too; they have nothing better to do."

"They both can be avoided if you're not into them, but like anywhere, they can be found if you know what you want to do. **Punishment for breaking the rules is not so severe** and usually includes community service and fines."

"**Drinking fines are hefty**! And Villanova makes a lot of money from it."

"Campus is very strict. **The campus does not tolerate drinking or drug use on campus**. Students sneaking beer or liquor into their dorm rooms may be asked by Public Safety to show them the contents of their bags. You will never get in trouble for being drunk or high, unless you are drunk to the point of vomiting or passing out. Very often, students with weak stomachs have been taken to the hospital for alcohol poisoning. This trip is normally accompanied by hefty fines."

"Underage drinking and drug use of any kind are not tolerated. There are **many rules to enforce the notion of safety and good health** practices on campus, but like any university, there are going to be problems with both of these things."

"**Campus police are trying to do their jobs**. Students break the law, and Public Safety has to enforce it. Students get upset when they get in trouble, but they are breaking the law. Drinking, drugs, parties, and what-not do go on and aren't always punished. If kids aren't stupid about their social activities, they shouldn't run into problems."

"They are very strict with drugs and drinking. You will have to pay a fine, do community service, or get kicked out. In other words, **avoid the drugs at all costs**. Don't do anything stupid or experiment with drugs and drinking. This only leads to more problems if over-abused. The majority of the time, your RAs or Public Safety will catch you drinking and doing drugs, so watch out!"

"**Campus police are pretty strict** about drugs and drinking. There is a pretty hefty fine if a person is caught with alcohol, and it is pretty easy to be put on probation."

"The campus police are definitely not the people to run into if you are intoxicated in any way. For the most part, they will notice and then take action, and being written up is by no means good. **They will pretty much take whatever you have away**, then write you up, and then you go meet with the dean to determine consequences."

"The campus police are very strict about drugs and alcohol. **They will write you up** or refer you to local police if necessary."

"I have heard of **hundreds of dollars in fines for getting caught with beer in the room**. I think that the policies are a little too strict."

"I know people get written up, and there are fines, but **I don't think that the police are that strict about it**. You don't get expelled or anything."

The College Prowler Take On... Campus Strictness

While parking illegally, having candles in your dorm room, and playing hall sports are things that RAs and the campus police are strict about, the thing that can get you in the most trouble is drugs and alcohol. Villanova once carried the title of a party school, but the administration has taken steps over the years to make it more and more difficult for students to drink. If you are smart about it and you aren't noisy, you and your friends can have a fun night without running the risk of getting in trouble. However, if you get even remotely noisy, there is a good chance you're going to get caught. Any alcohol-related offense runs up a fine and a course in alcohol education, so it's better to avoid them completely.

The University carries strict penalties, but if you are smart and responsible, this won't happen often enough to worry about them. Remember to be careful about what you become involved with and think carefully about whether or not your actions are worth the consequences that will most likely follow. Most of the students on campus are smart and responsible enough to know the limits. For that reason, nothing ever really gets out of control.

C-

The College Prowler® Grade on

Campus Strictness: C-

A high Campus Strictness grade implies an overall lenient atmosphere; police and RAs are fairly tolerant, and the administration's rules are flexible.

Parking

The Lowdown On... Parking

Approximate Parking Permit Cost:
$50–$100 per year

VU Parking Services:
(610) 519-6990
www.publicsafety.villanova.edu/parking.html

Student Parking Lot?
Yes

Freshmen Allowed to Park?
No

Common Parking Tickets:
No Parking Zone: $15
No Permit Displayed: $15
Fire Zone: $50
Handicapped Zone: $50

Parking Permits

No freshman or sophomore is permitted to park on campus, unless there are extenuating circumstances. You can now apply online for a parking permit. Parking areas will generally be in Main Lot, unless you are a resident of West Campus.

Did You Know?

Best Places to Find a Parking Spot

Main lot

Good Luck Getting a Parking Spot Here!

Dougherty Drive

West Campus

While there is no requirement to pay tickets on campus, if you go to the school, you could be **withheld from graduation if you do not pay your parking fines**.

If you park without a permit or in a non-parking zone, you run the risk of having a nice **bright orange wheel lock** added to the décor of your car.

Students Speak Out On...
Parking

"Parking is decent. There are a few different lots to use. However, you can't have a car on campus until junior year. You don't really need one until then, either."

"**Parking in the main lot is easy**, but parking near the dorms or on West Campus is difficult."

"Only juniors and seniors are permitted to have cars on campus, unless there are special circumstances (jobs or doctor's appointments). **Parking in certain areas on campus is limited**, but the main parking lots always have spots."

"**You are not supposed to have a car until your junior year if you are living on campus**. There are always open parking spots around campus, though."

"Parking is a problem at Villanova, and they do not allow cars for freshmen because of a lack of spots, unless you have a reason for having a car. However, I don't have a car, and **I use public transportation** to get around town easily."

"There's **not much parking here**, but that's why freshmen and sophomores aren't allowed to have cars. I think that it's crazy that a teacher broke her foot, but was still unable to have a parking spot near her office. For a full-time employee, that's just insane."

"**It's easy to park, but hard to bring a car**. No freshmen or sophomores are allowed to have cars, but people find a way around this rule."

"It is **very difficult to park** and own a car on campus."

"**Freshmen and sophomores are only given parking permits for extraordinary purposes**, for example, if they have a medical condition and must drive regularly to a doctor. Parking can very often be a problem."

The College Prowler Take On...
Parking

Parking on campus is only a hassle junior year, when it's a battle to find a spot by the apartments. Since underclassmen can't bring cars onto campus, it helps alleviate any problems that could occur if everyone was to bring their car. While it's near impossible to find a spot on main campus, the main lot almost always has a few spots left over during the day. And at night, when the main lot clears out, anyone with a car should have no problem parking there.

Since you can't have a car on campus until your junior year, you get comfortable walking around campus to get from place to place. While parking may sometimes be a pain, particularly for the juniors living in the apartments, it is still a great help to have a car on campus. Most events, venues, and places to go tend to be out of walking distance from campus, and public transportation can become expensive. So even with the problems associated with parking, it never hurts to have a car around.

C-

The College Prowler® Grade on
Parking: C-

A high grade in the Parking section indicates that parking is both available and affordable, and that parking enforcement isn't overly severe.

Transportation

The Lowdown On... Transportation

Ways to Get Around Town:

On Campus

WildCat Shuttle (Blue Line)
(610) 519-6990 (for all shuttles)
Hours: Monday–Friday
8 a.m.–6 p.m.

Mobility Shuttle
(for disabled students)
Hours: Monday–Friday
9:30 a.m.–3 p.m.

Off Campus

WildCat Shuttle (White Line)
Hours: Monday–Friday
8 a.m.–6 p.m.

Off Peak Shuttle (White Line)
Hours: Monday–Friday
6 p.m.–1:30 a.m.

King of Prussia Mall Shuttle
Hours: Friday–Saturday
6 p.m.–12:30 a.m.

→

Public Transportation

Southeastern Pennsylvania Transportation Authority

(215) 580-7800

www.septa.com

Bus and train schedules are available at the Connelly Center Information Desk or the R7 and R100 stations.

Taxi Cabs

St. David's Taxi Service
(610) 688-2241

Bennett Taxi Service
(610) 525-1770

Car Rentals

Alamo
Local: (215) 492-3960
National: (800) 462-5266
www.alamo.com

Avis
Local: (215) 492-0900
National: (800) 331-1212
www.avis.com

Budget
Local: (215) 288-0263
National: (800) 527-0700
www.budget.com

Dollar
Local: (215) 365-4499
National: (800) 800-1000
www.dollar.com

Enterprise
Local: (610) 989-9924
National: (800) 261-7331
www.enterprise.com

Hertz
Local: (215) 492-7205
National: (800) 654-3131
www.hertz.com

(Car Rentals, continued)

National
Local: (215) 387-9077
National: (800) 227-7368
www.nationalcar.com

Best Ways to Get Around Town

King of Prussia Mall Shuttle

The R7 or R100 train lines

Ride from a friend

Walk

White Line Shuttle

Ways to Get Out of Town:

Airport

Philadelphia International Airport (PHL)

8000 Essington Ave.
Philadelphia

(215) 937-6937

www.phl.org

The Philadelphia International Airport is 21 miles and about a 25-minute drive from Villanova.

Airlines Serving Philadelphia

American Airlines
(800) 433-7300
www.aa.com

Continental
(800) 523-3273
www.continental.com

Delta
(800) 221-1212
www.delta.com

(Airlines, continued)

Northwest
(800) 225-2525
www.nwa.com

Southwest
(800) 435-9792
www.southwest.com

United
(800) 864-8331
www.united.com

US Airways
(800) 428-4322
www.usairways.com

How to Get to the Airport

Septa's R1 line from the 30th Street station costs about $18 round trip.

Villanova's SGA runs an airport shuttle a few days before each major break—for free. E-mails are sent a few weeks before with times and places.

A cab ride to the airport costs about $40.

Greyhound

Philadelphia Greyhound Trailways Bus Terminal

1001 Filbert St.
Philadelphia

(215) 931-4075

www.greyhound.com

The Greyhound Trailways bus terminal is in downtown Philadelphia, roughly 20 miles from campus.

Amtrak

Philadelphia 30th Street Train Station

30th and Market St.
Philadelphia

(215) 349-1069

www.amtrak.com

The Amtrak train station is in downtown Philadelphia, about 20 miles from campus.

Students Speak Out On... Transportation

"Public transportation is okay, but the off-campus shuttle is definitely convenient. This shuttle makes stops throughout campus and then continues on down Lancaster for several stops."

"**Septa (the trains and buses) is pretty good**. It does get annoying from time to time, because I always miss the train by one minute."

"The public transportation is very **convenient to get around town with a train, taxi, or bus**. It is very easy to find people to split cab fare with. I felt safe using the public transportation around Villanova, Philly, and the airport."

"The main public transportation is the Septa trains. You can get into Philly very easily on the train, but **the trains stop running at midnight**, so you have to take a cab back sometimes, which is expensive."

"**There are two train stations conveniently located** on campus. One of them is for more local destinations, and connects to a bus stop going even further around town. The other train goes up and down the Mainline, as well as into Philadelphia in about 30 minutes for just a few dollars. This one also connects in Philadelphia at 30th Street to Amtrak, making it a convenient way to get home for breaks."

"Villanova is luckier than most schools, because **it has the R5, which goes up the Mainline and into Philadelphia**."

"**Public transportation is very convenient, as we have two different train stops on campus**. Both take you into Philly, but into different parts, and one will eventually lead you to the King of Prussia Mall. I definitely take advantage of the trains, as I just took one into Philly to watch a court case for my business law class."

"It's easy to get around with public transportation, but after a while, it **gets to be too expensive** for just a quick trip."

"**There is an off-campus shuttle**, but I just think it's easier to walk or find someone with a car. If you can't walk there, it is a train distance or just too far away."

"There are two train stations right on campus. Both can bring you into Philadelphia in less than 30 minutes. There are also local buses, and Villanova runs a local shuttle as well. **You can get almost anywhere**, sometimes it just takes a little patience and planning ahead."

"**Villanova has two rail lines, the R5 and the R100**, with stops on campus. It's extremely easy to get into Philadelphia or the neighboring towns."

The College Prowler Take On...
Transportation

Villanova offers many convenient ways to get around without spending a lot of money. The shuttles on and off campus are a great service for students without a car who wish to hop to the next town over. The shuttles are reliable and almost always on time, so the students never have to worry about long waits. Transportation into Philly is just as easy, with two train lines and three train stations around campus to bring you there. It's under $10 round trip and under 30 minutes to the city. The only downfall is the city's subway system, which isn't well mapped out and can take a while to get used to. However, the regional rails running from the suburbs into the city are easy, cheap, and quick. There are also special shuttles that run to the airport before break, as well as a whole train line dedicated to traveling to and from the airport.

Whether it's a quick trip to the bookstore in Rosemont or a night in the city, there are varying ways of getting there and an affordable and convenient method of doing so. Public transportation may be daunting at first, but within a week or two, you'll have it down to a science.

B+

The College Prowler® Grade on

Transportation: B+

A high grade for Transportation indicates that campus buses, public buses, cabs, and rental cars are readily-available and affordable. Other determining factors include proximity to an airport and the necessity of transportation.

Weather

The Lowdown On...
Weather

Average Temperature:	
Fall:	56 °F
Winter:	33 °F
Spring:	52 °F
Summer:	74 °F

Average Precipitation:	
Fall:	11.69 in.
Winter:	10.39 in.
Spring:	12.35 in.
Summer:	12.72 in.

Students Speak Out On...
Weather

"Bring both warm-weather and cold-weather clothes. It can get very hot in the beginning and the end of the year. But, you can expect to see snow in the winter."

"The wonderful Northeast region provides its residents with **four distinct and moderate seasons**. Winter requires a good heavy coat for the many snow days we are almost guaranteed, while spring and fall are moderate with cool breezes and warm, sun-filled days."

"The weather is mild in the spring and fall, and winters can be cold. **Just bring some heavy sweaters and jackets for the winter**, and you'll be fine."

"The weather is cold and snowy during the winters, but nothing too bad. It is hot and sunny at the beginning and end of the school year. So, you should **bring all kinds of clothing that will keep you warm for the winter**. You can't go wrong with jeans and fashionable clothes."

"The **weather is cold and unpredictable**. It's warm in the fall until November and December when you need a jacket. If you are from the east coast, you expect it, if you are from the west, be prepared!"

"The **weather is typical for the east coast**. There are all four seasons, so bring some of everything."

"**You really have to bring all types of clothing**—warm clothes for winter and light clothes for the spring are a must."

"All four seasons are experienced here at Villanova. **Bring a raincoat and an umbrella**! You won't be sorry. Also, boots are a necessity in the winter for the slush and snow."

"The weather is good. There should be no worries. I come from Long Island, and it's pretty much the same. **There are four seasons**, so bring a nice warm jacket for winter."

"The weather is pretty mild. In the beginning of the year, it can get hot, in the 80s or so, and then in the winter, it gets down into the 20s and 30s on average. **Definitely bundle up in the winter**, though, then break out those shorts in the spring."

The College Prowler Take On...
Weather

The weather is typical of any mid-Atlantic state. Fall and spring are always nice and sunny with a light breeze, and the temperatures are in the upper 50s to mid 60s. Winters get cold for almost anyone's standards, and at least one big snowstorm occurs—but that usually turns into more fun than most parties. During big snowstorms you're guaranteed to see makeshift sleds out of pizza boxes and trays, not to mention snowball fights and snowmen. The only time it's really hot is during orientation, and unless you are in the older dorms, there is always air-conditioning.

If you are having trouble packing for school, a perfect gauge for what you should bring to campus is the vacation breaks. When you first arrive, shorts and T-shirts are a must, as it can be hot. However, during fall break, start to bring summer clothes home and fill your school closet with warmer clothes, light sweaters, and windbreakers. Over Thanksgiving break, get your winter wardrobe because it gets cold pretty quickly and doesn't let up until spring break. That's a perfect time to start bringing back warmer clothes, and by Easter break, you should be back to where you started. Some good ideas are waterproof boots for both the rain and snow, as well as a warm jacket and a good pair of gloves.

B-

The College Prowler® Grade on

Weather: B-

A high Weather grade designates that temperatures are mild and rarely reach extremes, that the campus tends to be sunny rather than rainy, and that weather is fairly consistent rather than unpredictable.

VILLANOVA UNIVERSITY

Report Card Summary

B+	ACADEMICS	A-	GUYS
B-	LOCAL ATMOSPHERE	A	GIRLS
A	SAFETY & SECURITY	A-	ATHLETICS
B+	COMPUTERS	B	NIGHTLIFE
B	FACILITIES	B	GREEK LIFE
B+	CAMPUS DINING	B+	DRUG SCENE
A-	OFF-CAMPUS DINING	C-	CAMPUS STRICTNESS
B	CAMPUS HOUSING	C-	PARKING
A-	OFF-CAMPUS HOUSING	B+	TRANSPORTATION
D+	DIVERSITY	B-	WEATHER

Overall Experience

Students Speak Out On... Overall Experience

"Villanova has been a really positive experience. It gets better every year. The people are really warm and energetic. I wouldn't want to be anywhere else."

"I love Villanova in **every facet that this school offers**. I have numerous friends from high school who go here. I enjoy the challenges of the classes, meeting new people, and my independence from home. There is no other university that I wish to attend besides Villanova!"

"**I love Villanova**. The people are smart and interesting, and there's always something to do—if you look for it. Go 'Nova!"

"I love Villanova so far, and after completing this first year, **I'm very happy with my experience**."

"I enjoy Villanova so far, and from what I hear, it only gets better. Villanova may not be as crazy as some of the schools that your buddies may go to, but it is still a lot of fun. **Join some sort of team or group to meet people fast**."

"If I had the option, **I would never leave Villanova**. Studying abroad was so difficult for me, but only because I didn't want to leave campus and miss all the great things that go on here everyday. There is no place in the world that I would rather be going to school. I am so happy that I found my college home here. Villanova really gives you the opportunity to make something real of yourself, to find who you are and what you can become by exploring the world and experiencing all facets of it."

"I love Villanova, and I could not have asked for a better school. Some people may have a few qualms about the school, but if you go to any school, you will have that small group who does. **The class sizes are wonderful**, the spirit at basketball games is crazy, and everyone on campus is just so nice. You can even walk into the bathroom after just waking up and have a conversation with the cleaning lady or wave to the men outside working on the landscaping. Everyone is so nice and accommodating."

"I have seriously considered transferring enough to the point that I have applied to other schools. It's hard because all of the upperclassmen rave over the school, and I was not experiencing any of that love. By the end of the first semester, I was tired of having to wait, because all of my friends from other schools were immediately having the best time of their lives. **Every school has its pros and cons**, and it is up to you to decide what is important before you have high expectations and then just set yourself up for disappointment."

"**My Villanova experience has been wonderful**. I love the school and all it has to offer. I enjoy being close to a city, but having a neighborhood feel. It's a good size, so I recognize faces without getting bored. I think that I am getting a wonderful education that I will be able to apply directly to the working world. I enjoy the people and the community that has been developed over the years at Villanova."

"I have had a decent experience so far at school. **I had no idea I had to take so many requirement classes**. My friends at other schools complain that they have four classes—well, I have six. There is not much fun on weekends, and it is surprising how many parents come visit each weekend. I have met some very cool people here, though."

"Villanova is not a real college deal. **It is too Catholic, too strict, and too homogenous**. I am thinking about transferring, but find cool people who are like you, and you are golden!"

"My first semester, I was appalled by the lack of diversity on campus, the anemic party scene, and the political apathy at Villanova. I have transfer applications to Columbia, NYU, and UPenn. However, I believe I'll receive just as good, if not better, education here. I'll never be taught by a TA at Villanova. The **party scene picks up as you know more people**, especially more upperclassmen. Politically, I'm on the executive board of the Villanova Democrats now. So, I'll probably stay."

The College Prowler Take On...
Overall Experience

Villanova is a school that grows on you—for some it takes only until the end of orientation, for others it takes two semesters or more. Whatever the case, students get caught up in what it means to be a Villanovan and to be from the 'Nova nation. Villanova provides students with an excellent education, well enough to confidently put alumni head-to-head with Ivy grads and be successful. Outside its rich academic tradition, the students at Villanova come to know and appreciate their fellow students, professors, and surrounding community.

Going to the University gives students a unique perspective on college life. Even with a lack of diversity and a party scene that doesn't start to pick up until you are a junior, Villanova is a fun place to be. Villanova will not give you the typical college life of a wild youth, but regardless, it is a school that is both full of good times and exciting. While that might not be what someone is looking for, the students that do attend end up loving the school for everything it offers, from its basketball games and rich traditions, to its Catholic heritage and the full load of academics. It's a school that you can grow into comfortably, and looking back in later years, are glad to call your home away from home.

The Inside Scoop

The Lowdown On... The Inside Scoop

Villanova Slang:

Know the slang, know the school. The following is a list of things you really need to know before coming to Villanova. The more of these words you know, the better off you'll be.

Cam-Co/C Squared – Names for the Campus Corner.

C&F – Commerce and Finance, our business school.

CASA – An acronym to group Corr Hall, Austin Hall, St. Rita's, and Alumni dorms.

CEER – Center for Engineering Education and Research.

Chemies – Chemical Engineering students.

Chip Money/Cash to Chip – Money you can place on your WildCard that is stored on a chip, used to purchase items from the vending machines or just to do your dirty laundry.

The Courts – A group of off-campus housing in Bryn Mawr, it is very popular for Villanova students, as well as a site for a party or two on the weekends.

→

The Grotto – The area behind Alumni Hall.

Harcum – A college from which Villanova rents out a dorm for students not housed on the campus.

IK – The Italian Kitchen.

Mainline – Lancaster Ave.

The Make-out Tree – A huge tree that looks a lot like a weeping willow on Main Campus that is hard to see into when it has leaves.

Meal Plan – A unit that you can charge to get an amount of food designated by dining services as a meal.

Mendel Field – A large open field between Tolentine, White, and Mendel.

Motown – Mority Hall, a dorm off of main campus.

The Oreo – Central meeting spot right outside Connelly, a piece of modern art that looks a lot like an Oreo.

P&J – Peace and Justice Department.

PIT – The name for the cafeteria in the basement of Dougherty Hall.

Points – Amounts of points are given to you along with your meal plan, and they can be used like cash in any of the dining services restaurants or cafeterias.

The Quad – Sheehan and Sullivan dorms.

R5 – The SEPTA train line that runs directly into Philadelphia's 30 Market Street station.

R100 – The SEPTA light rail line that runs into west Philadelphia.

Sheehan Beach – The large field behind Sheehan.

SOD – An acronym to group Simpson, O'Dwyer, Delurey dorms on Main Campus.

SPIT – The name for the cafeteria on South Campus.

WildCard – The student ID.

Things I Wish I Knew Before Coming to Villanova

- Get on the smallest meal plan possible.
- Sign up for mailing lists, and go to meetings when you can.
- Offering cookies is a great way to meet new people.
- Unless you are in C&F, don't buy your computer through the school.
- It's not a big party school.
- Take as many AP tests as possible; it's much better to spend $80 than $570.
- Only freshmen wear lanyards backwards or in their shirts.
- How to manage my time better.
- Sign up for the Around Philadelphia tour in the acceptance packet.

Tips to Succeed at Villanova

- Pick classes you actually like.
- Research your professors before choosing your classes.
- Actually go to class.
- E-mail your professors, and let them know you'll be in their class.
- Check your e-mail at least 10 times a day.
- Do your homework yourself so you understand the material.
- Get to know your professors—stay after class and chat.
- Always dispute bad grades.
- Have an idea of what you want to take for a major.

Villanova Urban Legends

- St. Mary's is haunted by an assortment of ghosts.
- *Playboy* ranked Villanova the fifth hottest campus in America.
- There's a secret tunnel under St. Mary's that leads to a statue on Main Campus.

School Spirit

Varying in response, depending on who you ask, there will always be a common theme of students at Villanova: they are proud of where they go. While school spirit is not a 24-hour thing, it shows up for the important events like the University of Delaware football game and the basketball game against Saint Joseph's University. To get a sample of what it's like, just walk around campus to see the bundles of Villanova gear, ranging from the ever fashionable flip-flops to the casual sweatshirts. The few rivalries among organizations on campus also aid in the overall school spirit, for most see themselves as a student, not a Greek-life member or College of Liberal Arts student. Students are proud to bear the name of Villanova, and few will talk badly about the school in front of anyone outside the school.

Traditions

Dorm Olympics

Early year, Inter-Hall Council gives you the opportunity to show your dorm pride and compete with all the other dorms on campus for the title of the best dorm. Collecting a group of friends, students engage head-on with the other dorms for honor and pride. Kicking it off with a torch-lighting ceremony, teams compete in events ranging from tug-of-war to sumo wrestling in big, overstuffed suits. Interspersed among the events are a huge barbeque, music, cotton candy, and other fun stuff.

Freshmen Orientation Ceremony

At the completion of freshmen orientation every year, students and orientation counselors pack into the Pavilion for a very moving ceremony. After a few speeches by assorted administrators and guest speakers, all the students are given a candle. Then, one by one, each student lights the person's candle next to them until everyone in the freshman class has a lit candle. After singing the alma mater, the candles are blown out again until senior year when the same class comes together again in the Pavilion for the same ceremony that started it all.

(Traditions, continued)

Greek Week

A tradition mostly exclusive to Greeks, it is a weeklong competition with different events held around campus to select the number one fraternity and sorority for the year. Each day of events have point values, and at the end of the week all the points are tallied up to find the winner.

Homecoming Weekend

Held in the fall, Homecoming is a chance for alumni and students to get together and have a good time. Sheehan Beach is closed down to anyone under 21, but if you are of age, it's free beer all day. There are barbeques before the football game, and it's probably the most popular and fun football game of the season.

Men's Basketball Games

No matter if you are a fan of basketball or not, one thing not to be missed is the men's basketball games. Outside the heated competitive games against school rivals, the games themselves are a great way to get a feel about the community of Villanova. Alumni and students alike all share in traditions that have been around since the start of the team. Some examples are that at every home game, the team runs down the student section before going on the court, or at the end of the game, win or lose, the team faces the student section and together everyone sings the alma mater.

Pennsylvania Special Olympics

Every year for the last 16 years, Villanova has been home to the Pennsylvania Special Olympics. While it is supposed to be for the players involved, Villanova students get into it as much as the competitors and parents do. Different games are held all over campus, and it's never hard to spot a group of passing students that decided to stay and cheer on the teams. Beyond that, about half the campus actively participates in putting it together, whether it's running the opening ceremonies or making sure the teams are where they need to be, it's not hard to be caught up in the enthusiasm the athletes bring to the games.

(Traditions, continued)

Saint Thomas of Villanova Day

In honor of the school's patron saint, Saint Thomas of Villanova, every September students have an abbreviated class day, followed up by a mass, a parade, and then a huge barbeque. Before mass, students, administrators, and the Augustinians line up outside the church and head over to the Pavilion for convocation and then onto Sheehan Beach, where there are huge barbeque pits and free food for all students.

Senior Week

After everyone's packed up and gone home, the graduating seniors stay behind for a week of memories and fun. During the week, seniors attend numerous award ceremonies, banquets, and cocktails honoring their last four years at Villanova. On the weekend is the Pub Crawl, where seniors organize into large groups and bounce from bar to bar for most of the weekend in a final farewell.

Finding a Job or Internship

The Lowdown On... Finding a Job or Internship

Career Center:
Career Services Office
Corr Hall
(610) 519-4060
www.villanova.edu/vpaa/careers

Grads Entering the Job Market:
Within 6 Months: 68%
Within 1 Year: N/A
Within 2 Years: N/A

Services Available:
Career conferences and fairs
Career counseling
Career library
Graduate school advising
Mock interviews
NovaNet mentoring
Online job postings
Placement advising
Reference letters
Resumes and cover letters

Firms That Most Frequently Hire Graduates

Children's Hospital of Philadelphia, Deloitte, Ernst & Young, Goldman Sachs, Hospital of University of Pennsylvania, KPMG, Lockheed Martin, Merrill Lynch, Morgan Stanley, PricewaterhouseCoopers, U.S. Navy, The Vanguard Group, Villanova University

Advice

If you are thinking about getting a job after school and are worried that you aren't going to find one, you're not alone. And that's why Villanova's Career Services is there to help. While Career Services will do all it can for you, it is still important to get out there and network within the field you're after.

Right after orientation is over, don't feel awkward about taking a short walk to the Career Service's building and see what they have to say. They can help you figure out a major and career path, find employment on or off campus, or help refine your career goals. Getting a head start never hurts and can only help you out in the future.

Average Salary Information

College of Arts	**$33,413**
Communications	$31,765
Economics	$40,291
Education	$38,185
English	$30,970
History	$27,266
Honors	$32,500
Human Services	$29,583
Liberal Arts	$40,430
Philosophy	$32,938
Political Science	$33,942
Psychology	$29,700
Sociology	$36,250
Spanish	$32,500

(Average Salary Information, continued)

College of Science	**$39,005**
Astronomy	$32,900
Biology	$32,230
BSC	$35,608
Chemisty	$33,725
CSC	$43,720
Mathematics	$42,786
College of Commerce and Finance	**$42,836**
Accounting	$43,721
Business Administration	$58,250
Economics	$39,125
Finance	$43,724
MIS	$41,031
Management	$37,091
Marketing	$36,907
College of Engineering	**$46,836**
Civil Engineer	$43,469
Chemical Engineer	$49,575
Computer Engineer	$50,184
Electrical Engineer	$47,424
Mechanical Engineer	$43,531
College of Nursing	**$51,848**

Alumni

The Lowdown On... Alumni

Office:
Alumni House
800 Lancaster Ave.
www.villanova.edu/advance/alumni
alumni@villanova.edu

Services Available:
Alumni license plates
Career Services
Communication services
Corporate partners
Credit card
Hotel discounts
Insurance
Networking

Major Alumni Events

The biggest events for alumni are Homecoming, basketball games, and class reunions. Homecoming takes place in the fall and features a football game and other events previously listed. Basketball games are throughout the winter with attendance made up mostly by alumni; class reunions take place year round, and can be found on the alumni Web site.

Did You Know?

?

Villanova has had an **alum participating in every summer Olympics** since 1948, eight of which were gold medal winners.

Famous Villanova Alumni

Jim Croce (Class of '65) – singer, songwriter and musician, his most famous song is "Bad, Bad Leroy Brown"

Andy Allen (Class of '77) – former NASA astronaut, orbited earth in the space shuttle Atlantis

John Rowland (Class of '79) – former Connecticut governor

Edward Pinckney (Class of '85) – former NBA player, inducted into the Villanova Hall of Fame

Sonia O'Sullivan (Class of '91) – Gold medallist, 5,000 meter sprinter for team Ireland

Kerry Kittles (Class of '96) – NBA guard

Brian Westbrook (Class of '00) – NFL running back, currently plays for the Philadelphia Eagles

Student Organizations

Academic/Professional

Academic Competition Club

Accounting Society

ACM - Association for Computing Machinery

Advertising Society

AIChE - American Institute of Chemical Engineers

ASCE - American Society of Civil Engineers

ASME - American Society of Mechanical Engineers

Astronomical Society

Book Club

C&F Peer Counselors

Career Assistants

Chemistry Society

Computer Hardware Club

Concrete Canoe

Debate Society

Ecological Society

Economic Society

EJC - Engineering Joint Council

Engineering Peers

Engineers without Borders

Entrepreneurial Society

Equity Society

Ethics Society

FMA - Financial Management Association

Graduate Nurse Network

Graduate Student Council

History Club

Human Powered Submarine

Human Powered Vehicle

Institute of Electrical and Electronics Engineers

IBS - International Business Society

(Academic/Professional, continued)

International Relations Club/ Model UN

Literary Society

Macintosh Users Group

Management Society

Marketing Society

Mathematicians Club

Mini-Baja

NSBE - National Society of Black Engineers (VUMES)

NSCS - National Society of Collegiate Scholars

Organization of Human Services

Peer Mentors for Liberal Arts & Sciences

PA State Education Association

Phi Beta Lambda

Philosophy Graduate Studies Union

Physics Society

Pre-Law Society

Society for Human Resource Management

Society of Women Engineers

Sports Marketing Association

Steel Bridge Team

SNAP - Student Nurses Association of Pennsylvania

Teach for America

Undergraduate Nursing Senate

Whiskey Company (NROTC Drill Team)

Women in Business

Writers Club

Athletic

Club Basketball (W)

Club Crew (M)

Club Lacrosse (M)

Club Lacrosse (W)

Club Soccer (M)

Club Soccer (W)

Club Volleyball (M)

Club Water Polo (M)

Cycling Club

Equestrian Club

Golf Club

Ice Hockey Club (M)

Intramurals

Judo Club

Karate Club

Running Club

Sailing Club

Ski & Snowboard Club (VSSX)

Ski Team

Surf Club

Table Tennis Club

Tennis Club

Ultimate Frisbee Club (W)

Villanova Adventure Group

Villanova Ultimate Frisbee

Cultural

African Students Association

Arabic Cultural Society

Armenian Youth Organization (AYO)

Asian Student Association (ASA)

Black Cultural Society (BCS)

Caribbean Student Association

(Cultural, continued)

Chinese Club

Chinese Student Association

French Club

German Club

Hellenic Cultural Club

Hillel

Hispanic Society

Indian Student Association

Irish Cultural Society

Italian Club

Japanese Club

Latino American (LASO)

Multicultural Students League

Muslim Student Association

Native American Student Association

Polish Cultural Club

South Asian Multicultural Organized Students Association (SAMOSA)

Spanish Club

Student Association for Villanovan International Awareness

Honors Societies

Alpha Epsilon Delta (Pre-Med)

Alpha Sigma Lambda (University College)

Beta Alpha Psi (Business)

Beta Beta Beta (Biological)

Beta Gamma Sigma (C & F)

Chi Alpha Epsilon (Multicultural)

Chi Epsilon (Civil Engineering)

Delta Phi Alpha (German)

(Honors Societies, continued)

Eta Kappa Nu (Electrical Engineering)

Gamma Phi (Business)

Gamma Sigma Epsilon (Chemistry)

Gamma Theta Upsilon (Geography)

Kappa Delta Pi (Graduate Education)

Lambda Pi Eta (Communication Arts)

Omicron Delta Epsilon (Economics)

Omicron Delta Kappa (Leadership)

Order of Omega

Pi Alpha Theta (History)

Phi Beta Kappa (Arts Science)

Phi Kappa Phi (Interdisciplinary)

Phi Sigma (Biology)

Phi Sigma Tau (Philosophy)

Pi Delta Phi (French)

Pi Mu Epsilon (Mathematics)

Pi Sigma Alpha (Poli Sci)

Pi Sigma Epsilon (Marketing)

Pi Tau Sigma (Mechanical Engineering)

Psi Chi (Psychology)

Sigma Delta Pi (Spanish)

Sigma Pi Sigma (Physics)

Sigma Theta Tau (Nursing)

Sigma Xi (Scientific Research)

Tau Beta Pi (Engineering)

Theta Alpha Kappa (Religion)

Upsilon Pi Epsilon (Computer Science)

Media

Arthology (Literary Magazine)

Belle Aire Yearbook

CONCEPT - Graduate Studies

Polis (Literary Magazine)

Tech Crew

The *Villanova Engineer*

The *Villanova Times*

WVTV

The *Villanovan*

WXVU 89.1 FM

Music and Dance

Capoeira

Dance Company

Dance Ensemble

Dance Team

Flags/Silks

Gospel Choir

Haveners (Female Acappella)

Jazz Ensemble

Music Activities Stage Crew

Nova Dhadkan

Nova Jhoom

Orchestra

Pastoral Musicians

Pep Band

Spires (Male Acappella)

String Ensemble

Student Musical Theatre

Supernovas

Twirlers

Villanova Student Theatre

Villanova Singers (Male)

Villanova Voices (Female)

Vocal Minority (Acappella)

Peace and Justice

Amnesty International

Bread for the World

Environmental Group

Feminist Coalition

Global AIDS

Good Schools

Hunger & Homelessness Awareness Week

International Coalition Against Racism

Operation Smile

Progressive Student Network

UNICEF

Villanovans For Life

Political

College Democrats

College Republicans

Democracy Matters

Villanova Civil Liberties Association

Service

Alex's Lemonade Stand

Alpha Phi Omega

Balloon Day

Best Buddies

Bigs and Littles

Habitat for Humanity

Handicapped Encounter Christ

Movement Against Cancer

Random Acts of Kindness

Rays of Sunshine

Special Olympics

Up 'Til Dawn

Special Interest:

Auto Club
Basketball Club
Billiards Club
CAT – Campus Activities Team
Chess Club
Club CHAT
Color Guard
DDR
The Didge
Electronic Gamers Association (VEGO)
Formula SAE
Gay-Straight Coalition
Interfaith Coalition
Inter-Hall Council
Japanese Animation Club (VUJAC)
Knit and Crochet Club
Manga and Graphic Novel Club
Midshipmen Society
Military Ex Comp
Mock Trial
NovaFest
Photography Club
PRSSA
Pugwash
Robotics Club
Semper Fidelis
Senior Activities Committee
START – Student Alumni Relations Team
Student Art League of Villanova
Thundercats

University Service:

Ambassadors
Blue Key Society
New Student Orientation
PASS – Peers Advocating Substance Safety
POWER – Peers Offering Wellness Education & Resources
SGA – Student Government Association
VEMS – Villanova Emergency Medical Services

The Best & Worst

The Ten BEST Things About Villanova

1. The students
2. The Oreo
3. Basketball games
4. Philly cheesesteaks
5. The Villanova movie channel
6. Location
7. The junior apartments
8. The R5 and the R100
9. Sheehan Beach
10. Free movies at the cinema

The Ten **WORST** Things About Villanova

1. No diversity
2. The freshman visitation policy
3. Main Campus dorms
4. Radnor police
5. The walk from West to South Campus
6. Satellite gyms
7. Fire drills
8. Everything closes at 10 p.m.
9. No Greek housing
10. Strictness concerning alcohol

Visiting

The Lowdown On... Visiting

Hotel Information:

Philadelphia:

Four Points by Sheraton
4101 Island Ave.
Philadelphia
(215) 492-0400
www.sheraton.com
Distance from Campus:
20 miles
Price Range: $79–$120

Hampton Inn
8600 Bartram Ave.
Philadelphia
(215) 966-1300
www.hamptoninn.com
Distance from Campus:
20 miles
Price Range: $145–$170

Holiday Inn
4100 Presidential Blvd.
Philadelphia
(215) 477-0200

→

(Holiday Inn, continued)

www.holiday-inn.com

Distance from Campus:
6 miles

Price Range: $118–$190

Residence Inn by Marriott

191 Washington St.
Conshohocken

(610) 828-8800

www.marriott.com/residenceinn

Distance from Campus:
5 miles

Price Range: $119–$229

Mainline:

Courtyard

762 W. Lancaster Ave.
Wayne

(610) 687-6633

www.marriott.com/courtyard

Distance from Campus:
4 miles

Price Range: $89–$199

The Desmond

1 Liberty Blvd.
Malvern

(610) 296-9800

www.desmondgv.com

Distance from Campus:
13 miles

Price Range: $109–$329

Radnor Hotel

591 E. Lancaster Ave.
St. David's

(Radnor Hotel, continued)

(610) 688-5800

www.radnorhotel.com

Distance from Campus:
Less than a mile

Price Range: $99–$199

Wayne Hotel

139 E. Lancaster Ave.
Wayne

(610) 687-5000
(800) 962-5850

www.waynehotel.com

Distance from Campus:
2 miles

Price Range: $139–$169

King of Prussia and Valley Forge:

Best Western

127 S. Gulph Rd.
King Of Prussia

(610) 265-4500

www.bestwestern.com

Distance from Campus:
6 miles

Price Range: $85–$105

Comfort Inn

550 W. Dekalb Pike
King of Prussia

(610) 962-0700

www.comfortinn.com

Distance from Campus:
10 miles

Price Range: $99–$109

The Great Valley House Bed and Breakfast
1475 Swedesford Rd.
Malvern
(610) 644-6759
www.greatvalleyhouse.com
Distance from Campus: 8 miles
Price Range: $95–$120

Motel 6
815 W. Dekalb Pike
King of Prussia
(610) 265-7200
www.motel6.com
Distance from Campus: 8 miles
Price Range: $50–$70

Radisson Hotel
1160 First Ave.
King of Prussia
(610) 337-2000
www.radisson.com
Distance from Campus: 9 miles
Price Range: $109–$179

Wyndham Suites
888 Chesterbrook Blvd.
Wayne
(610) 647-6700
www.wyndham.com
Distance from Campus: 8 miles
Price Range: $87–$129

Take a Campus Virtual Tour

www.admission.villanova.edu/virtualtour/index.html

To Schedule a Group Information Session or Interview

Call (610) 519-4000 on any weekday from 8:30 a.m. to 5 p.m. Eastern Time.

Group information sessions generally are held at 1 p.m. on the weekends and are followed by a tour of campus.

Campus Tours

Campus tours run most Mondays through Saturdays (except on holidays, between semesters and during finals). Tours depart at 10:30 a.m., 11:30 a.m., 2 p.m., and 3 p.m. Call in advance to check the availability of the tour!

Open Houses

A great way to familiarize yourself with the campus and see if this is the right school for you is to come to one of the open houses. Each college holds an open house in the fall where you can listen to administrators, teachers, and students from each of the colleges.

Important Tip

Even with the open house, tours, and information sessions, you may not receive an accurate portrayal of what Villanova has to offer. Don't be afraid to walk up to a random student around the Oreo or Connelly Center and ask if you could talk about the school for a few minutes. Most of the students would be more than happy to answer any questions you may have. It also offers a more accurate portrait of the school.

Directions to Campus

Driving from the North

- Take the NJ Turnpike (I-95) to Exit 6 (Pennsylvania Turrnpike 276).
- Follow the Pennsylvania Turnpike west to Exit 20 (I-476 South/Chester).
- Take I-476 South to Exit 13 (Villanova/St. David's).
- At the bottom of the ramp, turn right onto Rt. 30, also known as Lancaster Avenue.
- Stay in the right-hand lane until Villanova's main parking lot is visible to your right; it will be the fourth traffic light.
- Immediately turn right at the light into the parking lot.

Driving from the West

- Take the Pennsylvania Turnpike (I-76) to Exit 326 (Valley Forge).
- Follow Interstate 76 to Exit 331A (I-476 South/Chester).
- Take I-476 South to Exit 13 (Villanova/St. David's).
- At the bottom of the ramp, turn onto Rt. 30 East, also known as Lancaster Avenue.
- Stay in the right-hand lane until Villanova's main parking lot is visible to your right; it will be the fourth traffic light.
- Immediately turn right into the parking lot at the light.

Driving from the South

- Take Interstate 95 North to Exit 7 (I-476 (Blue Route) North-Plymouth Meeting).
- Take I-476 North to Exit 13 (Villanova/St. David's).
- At the bottom of the ramp, turn onto Route 30 East, also known as Lancaster Avenue.
- Take Lancaster Avenue four traffic lights down and at the last light, the main parking lot entrance will be on your right.

Driving from the East

- Take the NJ Turnpike (I-95) to Exit 6 (Pennsylvania Turnpike-276).
- Follow the Pennsylvania Turnpike west to Exit 20 (I-476 South/Chester).
- Take I-476 South to Exit 13 (Villanova/St. David's).
- At the bottom of the ramp, turn right onto Rt. 30, also known as Lancaster Avenue.
- Stay in the right-hand lane until Villanova's main parking lot is visible to your right; it will be the fourth traffic light.
- Immediately turn right at the light into the parking lot.

Words to Know

Academic Probation – A suspension imposed on a student if he or she fails to keep up with the school's minimum academic requirements. Those unable to improve their grades after receiving this warning can face dismissal.

Beer Pong/Beirut – A drinking game involving cups of beer arranged in a pyramid shape on each side of a table. The goal is to get a ping pong ball into one of the opponent's cups by throwing the ball or hitting it with a paddle. If the ball lands in a cup, the opponent is required to drink the beer.

Bid – An invitation from a fraternity or sorority to 'pledge' (join) that specific house.

Blue-Light Phone – Brightly-colored phone posts with a blue light bulb on top. These phones exist for security purposes and are located at various outside locations around most campuses. In an emergency, a student can pick up one of these phones (free of charge) to connect with campus police or a security escort.

Campus Police – Police who are specifically assigned to a given institution. Campus police are typically not regular city officers; they are employed by the university in a full-time capacity.

Club Sports – A level of sports that falls somewhere between varsity and intramural. If a student is unable to commit to a varsity team but has a lot of passion for athletics, a club sport could be a better, less intense option. Even less demanding, intramural (IM) sports often involve no traveling and considerably less time.

Cocaine – An illegal drug. Also known as "coke" or "blow," cocaine often resembles a white crystalline or powdery substance. It is highly addictive and dangerous.

Common Application – An application with which students can apply to multiple schools.

Course Registration – The period of official class selection for the upcoming quarter or semester. Prior to registration, it is best to prepare several back-up courses in case a particular class becomes full. If a course is full, students can place themselves on the waitlist, although this still does not guarantee entry.

Division Athletics – Athletic classifications range from Division I to Division III. Division IA is the most competitive, while Division III is considered to be the least competitive.

Dorm – A dorm (or dormitory) is an on-campus housing facility. Dorms can provide a range of options from suite-style rooms to more communal options that include shared bathrooms. Most first-year students live in dorms. Some upperclassmen who wish to stay on campus also choose this option.

Early Action – An application option with which a student can apply to a school and receive an early acceptance response without a binding commitment. This system is becoming less and less available.

Early Decision – An application option that students should use only if they are certain they plan to attend the school in question. If a student applies using the early decision option and is admitted, he or she is required and bound to attend that university. Admission rates are usually higher among students who apply through early decision, as the student is clearly indicating that the school is his or her first choice.

Ecstasy – An illegal drug. Also known as "E" or "X," ecstasy looks like a pill and most resembles an aspirin. Considered a party drug, ecstasy is very dangerous and can be deadly.

Ethernet – An extremely fast Internet connection available in most university-owned residence halls. To use an Ethernet connection properly, a student will need a network card and cable for his or her computer.

Fake ID – A counterfeit identification card that contains false information. Most commonly, students get fake IDs with altered birthdates so that they appear to be older than 21 (and therefore of legal drinking age). Even though it is illegal, many college students have fake IDs in hopes of purchasing alcohol or getting into bars.

Frosh – Slang for "freshman" or "freshmen."

Hazing – Initiation rituals administered by some fraternities or sororities as part of the pledging process. Many universities have outlawed hazing due to its degrading, and sometimes dangerous, nature.

Intramurals (IMs) – A popular, and usually free, sport league in which students create teams and compete against one another. These sports vary in competitiveness and can include a range of activities—everything from billiards to water polo. IM sports are a great way to meet people with similar interests.

Keg – Officially called a half-barrel, a keg contains roughly 200 12-ounce servings of beer.

LSD – An illegal drug, also known as acid, this hallucinogenic drug most commonly resembles a tab of paper.

Marijuana – An illegal drug, also known as weed or pot; along with alcohol, marijuana is one of the most commonly-found drugs on campuses across the country.

Major –The focal point of a student's college studies; a specific topic that is studied for a degree. Examples of majors include physics, English, history, computer science, economics, business, and music. Many students decide on a specific major before arriving on campus, while others are simply "undecided" until declaring a major. Those who are extremely interested in two areas can also choose to double major.

Meal Block – The equivalent of one meal. Students on a meal plan usually receive a fixed number of meals per week. Each meal, or "block," can be redeemed at the school's dining facilities in place of cash. Often, a student's weekly allotment of meal blocks will be forfeited if not used.

Minor – An additional focal point in a student's education. Often serving as a complement or addition to a student's main area of focus, a minor has fewer requirements and prerequisites to fulfill than a major. Minors are not required for graduation from most schools; however some students who want to explore many different interests choose to pursue both a major and a minor.

Mushrooms – An illegal drug. Also known as "'shrooms," this drug resembles regular mushrooms but is extremely hallucinogenic.

Off-Campus Housing – Housing from a particular landlord or rental group that is not affiliated with the university. Depending on the college, off-campus housing can range from extremely popular to non-existent. Students who choose to live off campus are typically given more freedom, but they also have to deal with possible subletting scenarios, furniture, bills, and other issues. In addition to these factors, rental prices and distance often affect a student's decision to move off campus.

Office Hours – Time that teachers set aside for students who have questions about coursework. Office hours are a good forum for students to go over any problems and to show interest in the subject material.

Pledging – The early phase of joining a fraternity or sorority, pledging takes place after a student has gone through rush and received a bid. Pledging usually lasts between one and two semesters. Once the pledging period is complete and a particular student has done everything that is required to become a member, that student is considered a brother or sister. If a fraternity or a sorority would decide to "haze" a group of students, this initiation would take place during the pledging period.

Private Institution – A school that does not use tax revenue to subsidize education costs. Private schools typically cost more than public schools and are usually smaller.

Prof – Slang for "professor."

Public Institution – A school that uses tax revenue to subsidize education costs. Public schools are often a good value for in-state residents and tend to be larger than most private colleges.

Quarter System (or Trimester System) – A type of academic calendar system. In this setup, students take classes for three academic periods. The first quarter usually starts in late September or early October and concludes right before Christmas. The second quarter usually starts around early to mid–January and finishes up around March or April. The last academic quarter, or "third quarter," usually starts in late March or early April and finishes up in late May or Mid-June. The fourth quarter is summer. The major difference between the quarter system and semester system is that students take more, less comprehensive courses under the quarter calendar.

RA (Resident Assistant) – A student leader who is assigned to a particular floor in a dormitory in order to help to the other students who live there. An RA's duties include ensuring student safety and providing assistance wherever possible.

Recitation – An extension of a specific course; a review session. Some classes, particularly large lectures, are supplemented with mandatory recitation sessions that provide a relatively personal class setting.

Rolling Admissions – A form of admissions. Most commonly found at public institutions, schools with this type of policy continue to accept students throughout the year until their class sizes are met. For example, some schools begin accepting students as early as December and will continue to do so until April or May.

Room and Board – This figure is typically the combined cost of a university-owned room and a meal plan.

Room Draw/Housing Lottery – A common way to pick on-campus room assignments for the following year. If a student decides to remain in university-owned housing, he or she is assigned a unique number that, along with seniority, is used to determine his or her housing for the next year.

Rush – The period in which students can meet the brothers and sisters of a particular chapter and find out if a given fraternity or sorority is right for them. Rushing a fraternity or a sorority is not a requirement at any school. The goal of rush is to give students who are serious about pledging a feel for what to expect.

Semester System – The most common type of academic calendar system at college campuses. This setup typically includes two semesters in a given school year. The fall semester starts around the end of August or early September and concludes before winter vacation. The spring semester usually starts in mid-January and ends in late April or May.

Student Center/Rec Center/Student Union – A common area on campus that often contains study areas, recreation facilities, and eateries. This building is often a good place to meet up with fellow students; depending on the school, the student center can have a huge role or a non-existent role in campus life.

Student ID – A university-issued photo ID that serves as a student's key to school-related functions. Some schools require students to show these cards in order to get into dorms, libraries, cafeterias, and other facilities. In addition to storing meal plan information, in some cases, a student ID can actually work as a debit card and allow students to purchase things from bookstores or local shops.

Suite – A type of dorm room. Unlike dorms that feature communal bathrooms shared by the entire floor, suites offer bathrooms shared only among the suite. Suite-style dorm rooms can house anywhere from two to ten students.

TA (Teacher's Assistant) – An undergraduate or grad student who helps in some manner with a specific course. In some cases, a TA will teach a class, assist a professor, grade assignments, or conduct office hours.

Undergraduate – A student in the process of studying for his or her bachelor's degree.

ABOUT THE AUTHOR

Writing this book has been a great time, and I have learned a lot. While it was a lot of work, it was all rewarding. I hope to continue writing at some level—whether it's for a newspaper or books—well into the future. I am pursuing a double major in political science and economics, and I'm loving it here. I am a northern New Jersey native and have lived here all my life. I really hope that you enjoyed the book, and above all, found it useful in selecting a college. I remember applying to college and hope this book eases the stress of the application process, touring, and pressure from parents. If you have any questions, comments, or want to know more about Villanova or writing, feel free to e-mail me.

Also, a book would not be a book without a section for dedications. First and foremost, I would like to thank my mom and dad, whose hard work, perseverance, and loving care helped me get to where I am today. Then, of course, there is my brother Kyle, who is the greatest sibling an older brother can ask for. I'd also like to thank Poppy, who has always been a source of guidance and tons of fun and laughs, Uncle Peter and Aunt Lisa, who are like a second set of parents who are always great to have around, and the family that is no longer with us but who have been a great source of inspiration to me. Lastly, I can't forget my friends at Villanova and home who have made my life that much more enjoyable. Without them, life would be very boring. And, of course, to all the people at College Prowler, for allowing me this unique and educational experience!

Sean Wright
authors@collegeprowler.com

The College Prowler Big Book of Colleges

Having Trouble Narrowing Down Your Choices?

Try Going Bigger!

Big book of Colleges '09
7¼" X 10", 1248 Pages Paperback
$29.95 Retail
978-1-4274-0005-5

Choosing the perfect school can be an overwhelming challenge. Luckily, our *Big Book of Colleges* makes that task a little less daunting. We've packed it with overviews of our full library of single-school guides—more than 280 of the nation's top schools—giving you some much-needed perspective on your search.

College Prowler on the Web

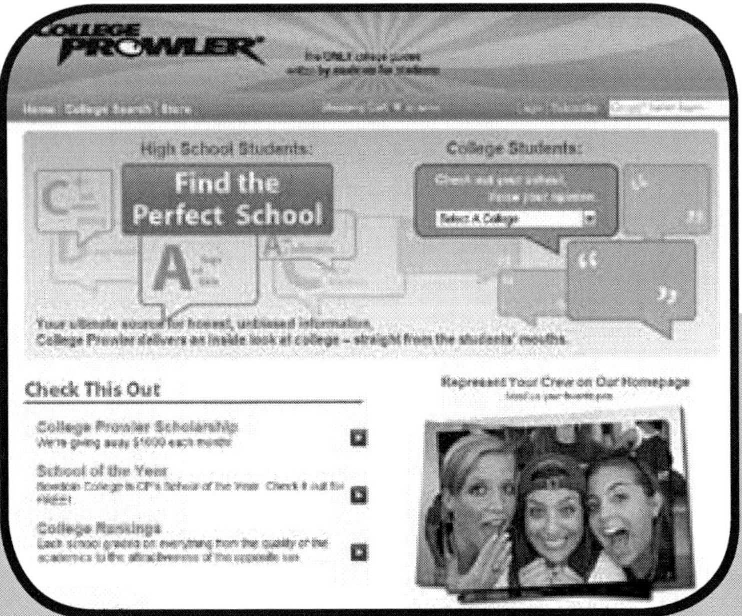

Craving some electronic interaction? Check out the new and improved **CollegeProwler.com**! We've included the COMPLETE contents of more than 250 of our single-school guides on the Web—and you can gain access to all of them for just $39.95 per year!

Not only that, but non-subscribers can still view and compare our grades for each school, order books at our online bookstore, or enter our monthly scholarship contest. Don't get left in the dark when making your college decision. Let College Prowler be your guide!

Pros and Cons

Still can't figure out if this is the right school for you? You've already read through this in-depth guide; why not list the pros and cons? It will really help with narrowing down your decision and determining whether or not this school is right for you.

Pros	Cons
....	....
....	....
....	....
....	....
....	....
....	....
....	....
....	....
....	....
....	....
....	....
....	....
....	....

College Prowler®

Pros and Cons

Still can't figure out if this is the right school for you? You've already read through this in-depth guide; why not list the pros and cons? It will really help with narrowing down your decision and determining whether or not this school is right for you.

Pros	Cons
....	....
....	....
....	....
....	....
....	....
....	....
....	....
....	....
....	....
....	....
....	....
....	....
....	....

COLLEGE PROWLER®

Notes

COLLEGE PROWLER®

Notes

Notes

COLLEGE PROWLER®

Notes

Notes

Notes

Notes

Notes

Notes

Notes

Notes

Notes

COLLEGE PROWLER®

Made in the USA